The Era of the Sons

Awakening the Sons of God

By

Brenda Lachelle Scarborough

Table of Contents

Forward iv

The Reign of His Glory 1

Volume One

Sandra's Story 3

Kallena's Story 12

Bishop's Story 21

Volume 2

Awakening the Sons of God 63

Volume 3

What Shall I Manifest 129

Forward

Brenda is a pastor who leads worship teams into the presence of God without apology. As I write this forward I feel a warm smile beginning to form. I know through the next few pages of this book you will be blessed; your life will never be the same. Brenda is a very gifted writer full of creativity and love. You will find her to be genuine, thoughtful, and pure. She is an extravagant and careful lover of God, who strives to please him more and more each day. She has the ability to tell it like it is as she has had her own near-death experience. Now she lives to tell her story.

Brenda is a powerhouse, of worship who sits at the Masters' feet to hear his love poured out for her. As you read these pages keep your heart open for what God will do for you. As He raised Brenda, He will raise you too. Be prepared to be blessed.

Bishop Ilinda Jackson
Secret Place Community Church

The Reign of His Glory

Volume One

Welcome to the Reign of His Glory. As the bride of Christ, I believe we are closer than we have ever been to understanding our full potential as children of God. In the next few entries of this book, I want to share some stories from friends who I have labored with in ministry. Over the years I have seen God move over and over again through their lives. Some have had to walk through tremendous amounts of grief and pain. Others have received miraculous healing while some have had to overcome rejection and failure. No matter what the test, one thing I can say about all of them is they have never given up and thrown in the towel. They kept pressing, kept moving when it was the hardest, darkest times in their lives. I hope these stories speak to you. One thing I want you to know and that I hope will become evident though these pages is that you never have to doubt God's love for you no matter what you are facing. You never have to live up to another standard, except what God requires of you. What do I mean by that? Comparing yourself to someone else is one of the biggest things that we do in society. We tend to make what God is requiring for another person a whole doctrine which we then think we must obey and uphold. We have more than 45,000 examples of denominations globally, but God is not interested in 'you building your own kingdom'. We are living in the time of Spirit and truth. I thought all the time I was waiting for God to bring me the tools to finish this fight well. I looked at verses like Romans 8:22-23 and I wanted to be that Son of God. The one who he uses to right everything wrong in the world. I thought I was waiting on God for an appointed time for me to walk in that fullness. As if it was one more thing he needs to give me in order for me to be a fully manifested son. Honestly, that is what this whole ten-year journey has been about. Up until two years ago I did not know that it was God who was waiting on me to finally understand who I really was and what I possess on the inside of me. I have everything that I need to be a fully manifested son in this earth, but it is up to me to be in a place where I can move from glory to glory and allow things to be revealed and unlocked within me. You see, that is why I said earlier we must live by the standards that God sets for us, and not compare ourselves. No matter where you are on the spectrum,

God is meeting you right there and walking at the pace that you set. I was entangled in rejection, depression, shame, and guilt. There are still areas in my life that are under construction. However, I know who I am, and it is being revealed more and more each day. God is unlocking the mysteries of what he has put on the inside of me. He is decluttering what has occupied space for so long and awakening me to a whole new realm. Welcome to the Reign of His Glory.

Sandra's Story

Day 1

There are just some people you meet and you immediately get attached to. That is Pastor Sandra or "Aunt Sandra" as I call her. During the first three years of knowing her she never let me drive her anywhere. Here we are five years into the relationship, in 2021, and I have had the privilege to do so many times now. You see, you must really understand what she has been through to know why I even mention that bit of information. Sandra has had to deal with and overcome what I would call some devastating situations through the course of her life. If she never told you her story you could never see that she has endured an incredible amount of grief. I think about my own life and given the same circumstances I would like to say I would be in a place of victory, but I cannot say that for sure. All I can say is that despite all the grief she has walked through, she has never given up and thrown in the towel. She has graciously allowed me to share her story with you in hopes that you are able to find the same kind of joy and peace she walks in today. When I tell you that she knows who she is, believe it.

At an early age Sandra had been abandoned and was left to be raised by her grandparents. She struggled with rejection and insecurities for years. Consequently, she says she probably was more over- protective with her children than most would have been. On July 4th, 1975, something Sandra never even imagined changed her life forever. After a day of fun at a local theme park with church family, Sandra had finally turned in for the night. This summer was the first time that Sandra's children (her loves as she calls them) were away from her. The family tradition, from when she grew up, was for all the grandchildren to go to Texas and spend the summer with the grandparents. This had been the first year that she had allowed her children to go and stay. Her daughter was eight and son was two and a half.

In Sandra's words: "3:30 a.m. on Saturday morning the phone rang, a call from a hospital in a small town in East Texas asking permission to treat my daughter. Of course, I gave permission, not knowing why she needed to be treated. I began to inquire. As the story unfolds, a head on collision with a station wagon and a pickup truck."

Not knowing where everyone was or the extent of everyone's injuries, Sandra found out that there were some fatalities with the accident. She started to call all the area hospitals that people might have been taken to. She knew that there were 13 people involved in the accident. Sandra was trying to find where her baby was taken. Her daughter was shaken up but okay with a few scrapes and bruises. She knew that one of her nieces was there with her daughter and had a broken arm. No one could tell her anything else. She finally found out that her father passed away from the car crash. Sandra called the funeral home in town where she knew they had taken her father and asked them if they had received a baby that night as a result of the car crash. She described what he looked like, and she received the dreaded news that her son did not make it. She was miles away but remembers her frame of mind and she says she really did not have time to react. She had to jump into action.

Day 1

Day 2

She learned that night her family had spent the holiday at the lake watching the fireworks. On the way home the car was filled with her family returning home from a day of fun. Her stepmother recalled the baby sitting with her stepsister in the back. Four other kids were asleep in the back of the station wagon and Sandra's father was riding in the passenger seat. Waiting to leave the lake, there was a line of cars in front of them. They were just a few miles away from home when her stepmother noticed a vehicle driving very strangely. A truck collided with them head on at full speed. The car accident made national news. That night six people lost their lives to a drunk driver. Her father, son, stepsister, sister's friend, and the two men in the truck died that night. What is amazing is the only way Sandra found out was that her daughter remembered her mother's phone number. There was no one else who would have been able to contact her so quickly. Her stepmother was in intensive care until after the funerals happened, not even knowing that she had lost her husband or daughter.

While telling me this story, I was amazed at the poise and strength that Sandra had when she said everyone else around her was falling apart. Sandra had her baby transferred back to Oklahoma and had the funeral on the next Tuesday. The very next day she was back in Texas at her father's funeral.

Sandra recalls the last interactions with her father and son. She remembers they stayed up all night talking, and she feels like her dad knew he was about to die simply because of the topics of their conversation that night. She remembers asking her baby if he wanted to come back with her and he said he wanted to stay with papa. This was one of the first times that he got to spend time with her dad. He was also excited about the other children who were around. She told me the morning that she left she got scared because as her son lay in the bed sleeping, he looked as if he was dead. She physically shook him to see if he was okay. She remembers driving off with her sister and wanting to turn around several times to go back for him. Walking through this tragedy there were several times Sandra thought to herself, "Why didn't I just go back to get him? Did I miss something God was trying to tell me? Could I have prevented this?"

A few years prior, Sandra was in her bed reading the bible one day and she came across Acts 16:31: *And they said, believe on the Lord Jesus Christ, and thou shalt be saved, and thy house.* Sandra said, "Lord, if this is true, save my daddy." Six months later she was visiting her father and to her surprise the Lord had done exactly what she asked him to do. After that he never touched another drink. This was two years before the accident. She explains how her father was saved and changed his life, how he spent the next few years helping build and repair the church he was buried in. Although Sandra missed her father, she was comforted in the fact that he knew Jesus. In fact, she credits her foundation in the faith to her late pastor who, months before she experienced this tragedy, began to teach them about death and life after death. Sandra told me that she believes had it not been for this teaching she would not have truly been able to cope and deal with what she had to walk through. But the question of 'what if' may always remain. What if she turned around and went back for her son? What if she never allowed him stay? She could have driven herself crazy with these questions. Just two years after that the Lord blessed her with another baby boy. During this time, she went through the lowest point of depression, because of her guilt from the death of her first son.

Day 2

Day 3

Life has a whole realm of uncertainties and fears. What I have noticed about her story is she has never looked at it as something that God did to her or was punishing her for. Her faith and trust in who he had already shown her he was, was the very thing that kept her grounded in the midst of tragedy. Over the years God has continued to uphold the promise of the words that Sandra held onto in Act 16 for her family. Many have been saved and reconciled. Most people like Sandra who have had such a horrible start in life never ever bounce back. It seems like circumstance after circumstance seems to keep them down. At an early age she had dysfunction in her life that could have made her a product of her environment. However, even as a child she can trace how the hand of God was always with her working all things for her good.

I think one of the biggest lacks we have in the church today is transparency. I never thought people dealt with the feelings they had nor emotional issues simply because they were never talked about. So, in keeping with this, I kept my feelings all inside and never dealt with them, thinking that there was something wrong with me. What if this was Sandra's place of origin? I mean, she certainly had the right, considering all that life had brought her. Maybe you are right here--you have tried the God thing and you feel somehow you do not measure up or can't get it right. Part of my issue was I could not see the truth; we teach about hearing the voice of God and knowing who he is. However, we are still a people with no vision. We lack the ability to see with the eyes of God. Reality is not what you are experiencing and going through at the moment. All of that is temporal and fleeting. God says those who worship him must do so in Spirit and in truth. We as Christians have all these cute understandings and mindsets of what that means. However, consider this for just a moment: I think we are living in those times. If you have no vision to see what is happening in the Spirit there is no way you can stand on God's truth. Notice I did not say truth, in fact you are standing on a place that you deem as truth, but is it God's truth? 2020 was certainly a trying year for the whole world; some people are still picking up the pieces today. About two years before, in 2018, Father God had really challenged me about increasing my vision to his vision. Unknowingly I was about to walk through one of the hardest years in my life. I will share my story a little later with you. Just as we say in Sandra's life, God has a way of preparing us for a place before we get there. Although she never would have chosen these circumstances, she has navigated these waters without giving up. She lives with hope and peace. All of what she has experienced has had a greater reward in her life than she could have ever expected. It has taken her to arenas where she has been able to relate and share the love of God to some who we would say are the unsavable. Her testimony has positioned her as a matriarch leader of her family. Her insight and revelation in prayer created a position within a company for her, where they pay her to pray and release insight and direction concerning the direction of the company. Everything she has accomplished or built has been based on her taking God at his word and believing his promises concerning her. That was her truth, what she has stood on over the years. This truth has never failed her.

Day 3

Kallena's Story

Day 1

When I met Kallena, there was something about the way she prayed. She gets lost in the presence of the Lord; nothing else even matters. It's as if there is no one there except her and God and is very personal and intimate. Kallena is truly an intercessor; working alongside her in ministry has taught me strength and resolve and assurance of the Lord. I feel honored to tell her story.

When she was 11, Kallena remembers being introduced to cancer for the first time. Her Aunt Brenda, who was 32 years old, died of breast cancer. She remembers being in her aunt's living room where a hospital bed was set up to care for her. Kallena's dad said, "She's not fighting, she's given up." You see, he knew exactly what cancer could do because he watched their mother die from it in her thirties, and their twin brothers both died from it when they were 13 years old. Now he stood, watching his sister go through the same thing. After her aunt passed away three of her four children came to live with her family. The oldest son was shot and killed one year later. The youngest of the daughters was diagnosed with breast cancer at 15. She went into remission for a while, later passing away at the age of 18 from cancer. Kallena remembers her cousin, the oldest daughter, and all she walked through with the amount of loss she had endured in her life. She turned to alcohol as a coping mechanism. She remembers having a conversation with her cousin, trying to encourage her. However, her cousin told her she knew she was "going to die early" just like everyone else. She died at the age of 27 from alcohol poisoning. Kallena said her father's biggest fear was to die from cancer, simply because of how he saw it ravage his family. At the age of 40 he passed away from cancer. Not only was there a history of cancer on her dad's side of the family, but her mom's side as well, as her grandmother died at 54 from cancer. Kallena also had a half-brother from her father that died at 13 from brain cancer.

Day 1

Day 2

Kallena went to a health fair and saw a booth that offered genetic screening for cancer. Knowing what her family history was she decided to sign up for it. The appointment was set for a couple of months out. One day she noticed a lump under her arm. It was not sore or hurting, just there. Kallena contacted her PCP and they told her not to worry about it but just to go to the appointment she already set up with the genetic testing people. "It's probably nothing to worry about," they said. When the appointment finally came, the doctor went through the history of her family before they did the exam and told her she more than likely had nothing to worry about since it was on her paternal side of the family. In Kallena's own words, "The doctor burst in the room and blurted out, "You have cancer." She remembers going to her car and crying as she called her mom to tell her the news. She kept thinking to herself, "I know what cancer can do." She had never seen anyone in her family live after being diagnosed with it. Sure, they went into remission, however, it always came back, and it was the thing that took them out. Kallena said at that moment, at the age of 32, she began to make her will and set things in order for her family which she was going to leave behind. Fear has a way of gripping us, and from her prospective there was no reason to hope simply because of what cancer had already done to her family. While interviewing Kallena I asked her, "Is this where you developed your fervency as an intercessor?" To my surprise she told me "No." Kallena was a teenage mother and by 22 she had all her five children already. She said things were hard being such a young mother. She remembers growing up in the Baptist church until she was about thirteen. When her mom switched to a Pentecostal church, Kallena said her mom didn't make her or her brother go to church. However, she remembers her mom over the years talking about the goodness and faithfulness of God. So, she decided to pursue a relationship herself. About three months into her seeking after God, she heard his voice for the first time, and he simply said, "Serve me." Kallena explains how she would be in her room seeking and praying for the presence of God to show up, and how it didn't matter if no one else in a service was into the worship--she found her place and reason to worship God even if nobody else wanted to. A little while after hearing God speak, he spoke again and this time he said, "You are filthy before me." She said God began to walk her through an account of what she needed to let go of and what did not please him about her. One of the things she leaned on in this journey was that he was more concerned about her character and integrity than anything else. She said he really began to teach her what that meant in her life. Remember I said earlier, you must understand how to live by the standards that God sets for you. Here is a perfect example of that. Kallena is a person of great integrity.

Just like Sandra, Kallena's foundation was set way before she walked through sickness. Kallena began the fight for her life still hopeful for victory, but she wavered back and forth with her faith. She said this was the place she finally learned how to divorce fear. This was the most powerful thing that I heard her say. Fear has a way of crippling our lives so that the very thing we fear can be the thing we end up manifesting. We must understand that we do have a choice; it is not entirely true that life doesn't give us a choice. We may not be able to control how life comes at us, but it is completely up to us with how we deal with it. I am not trying to make a religious stance here, but really hear my heart on this. Your mind is the most powerful gift you possess and how you rule with it determines the fruit you will receive. If you take God's true intent for your life and learn how to subdue and rule your mind, it is here that you open up a world of possibilities. Living in this place is where you were always called to live. What fruit do you want to manifest?

Day 2

Day 3

Kallena talked about how the Lord challenged her thinking, He asked her what she feared. The truth was death could have happened by anything that was beyond her control, not just cancer. As she went through chemo, she remembers working and still having to be a mother and wife. She had people all over the world praying for her and she believes that these prayers really held her up at her lowest points of faith. Kallena remembers one of the elders of the church saying to her, "Your kids are watching you." That really stuck with her and helped her make up her mind that no matter if she lived or died it would be for God. She said to herself, "For God I live and for God I die." She did not want her kids to be stuck in the same mindset of devastation that her cousin was stuck in, unable to move on or turning to substance abuse or worse, being angry with God. One day she heard a sermon by Bishop Ilinda Jackson entitled "*Giants Were Meant to Die, Fortified Cities Were Supposed to Fall.*" This message changed how she fought. Kallena won her first battle with cancer one year later but it came back. This time, in the same place ,which is very rare; it was on the skin. She went through treatment again. Here is her experience in her own words.

> Once the 2nd diagnosis came… a transition took place. Divorcing fear through cancer transitioned my thought pattern and life from a servant that just knew Him and did things for Him to a true son whom He loved. I had proof because He healed me the 1st time, He spoke with me, strengthened me, got me through it. This time I allowed and invited Him to walk with me through cancer. I felt like Adam in the garden where God would walk and talk and share His mysteries and reveal His truths. It was a journey where I discovered who I am in Him and things I believe. He led and guided my every step! The timing of surgery, radiation, etc. was perfect. They did not shut down the insurance company until my very last week of radiation which allowed me to have insurance, money, and now time at home to heal and recover.
>
> While being on disability I began to utilize the keys and weapons we are taught in ministry. (Declarations, praying scriptures over yourself, courts of heaven, etc). I became an active participant not

> only for others but myself. I at first had the mindset... He will do it for others but certainly not me. I remember singing ALL the time 'I need thee oh I need thee.' I relied completely and totally on the Lord. He was and is always faithful; He walked me on the journey of cancer so I could see it and there I set up an altar for Him and call him Jehovah Rapha (The Lord who heals and makes every bitter experience sweet). I discovered new truths about Him and know Him in a more intimate way.

Today she is completely healed. Just as important, she has closed the generational door that has haunted her family. No longer does cancer have the right to take any more of her family members. She has surpassed the age of 40 which is how old her father was when he passed away, and is also older than her older brother who died suddenly at the age of 42. Both of these are milestones for her. One of the most important things I have learned from Kallena is how important it was for her to divorce fear. The bible says the phrase "Fear not" 365 times, one for every day of the year. God encourages us not to fear. What if Kallena had accepted the idea that this is just what happens in my family? What if she accepted the idea of death? Maybe your situation is not this dramatic, but think about it: Where have you just accepted the thought of death? It could be natural or spiritual; death can represent anything that is void of the truth of God. Can you dream again? Can you stretch your faith? Can you begin to have new vision? It is never too late. Let us live again and reawaken to a whole new world of possibilities. Kallena is no different than you or me. The same promises of healing and wholeness belong to you; they are your birthright. My prayer for you is that in all things you learn how to grow in stature spiritually and prosper as your soul prospers. Healing is yours, it is the children's bread, and that means Spirit, soul, and body. Not only did Kallena receive physical healing, but it affected every part of her; she had areas she was even unaware healing was needed. This opened the door for a greater testimony.

> [31] What, then, shall we say in response to these things? If God is for
> us, who can be against us? [32] He who did not spare his own Son,
> but gave him up for us all—how will he not also, along with him,
> graciously give us all things?[33] Who will bring any charge against
> those whom God has chosen? It is God who justifies. [34] Who then is
> the one who condemns? No one. Christ Jesus who died—more than

that, who was raised to life—is at the right hand of God and is also interceding for us. [35] Who shall separate us from the love of Christ? Shall trouble or hardship or persecution or famine or nakedness or danger or sword? [36] As it is written:
"For your sake we face death all day long; we are considered as sheep to be slaughtered."[a]
[37] No, in all these things we are more than conquerors through him who loved us. [38] For I am convinced that neither death nor life, neither angels nor demons,[b] neither the present nor the future, nor any powers, [39] neither height nor depth, nor anything else in all creation, will be able to separate us from the love of God that is in Christ Jesus our Lord. (Romans 8:31-38 NIV).

Day 3

Bishop's Story

Day 1

Words would never be able to express who or what Bishop Ilinda Jackson is to me. She is more than just my pastor or mentor. I have learned so much from her ability to lead and pull on every hidden thing in me. She has helped to cultivate the natural giftings and callings that are on the inside. The thing that amazes me the most about Bishop is her capacity. I have never seen anything like it. She has this endurance and patience that never gives up. Quitting is not in her DNA. As a leader, I always look for integrity and character which to me are the most important things to have. Bishop has challenged me in this area more than she will ever know. I have grown in maturity under the covering of her leadership. Through the hardest time in my life, she was constant and unchanging as I navigated my way through. For that I want to say thank you from the bottom of my heart. You will never know how much, your words, prayers, encouragement, time, support, validation, and mentoring have meant to me. I appreciate every hug, tear, and place you have so richly and freely sown in my life and every bit of wisdom that you have imparted to me. Thank you for your patience and love toward me. I really could not have asked for a better leader. I feel honored that you wanted to be a part of this project and even more that I get to tell some of your story.

One of the most famous scriptures is Psalm 139:14: *I will give thanks to You, because I am awesomely and wonderfully made; Wonderful are Your works, and my soul knows it very well. (NASB)* The problem is we do not believe it. Somehow, we struggle with the idea that we have worth, mostly because we live in a world where love is conditional. God freely gives his love, but our love works on a merit system.

Bishop Ilinda grew up in a very large family. She remembers the house always had some sort of background noise going on. She said she was raised in a very loving home and although her father did not live with them, she still had a relationship with him. She noticed an undertone at an early age. You could call it middle child syndrome because she is a middle child. Before she really knew what that was, she noticed she did not really fit in. Her older sisters were very beautiful, tall, and liked by everyone. Bishop Ilinda says she is not really sure what context this phrase was said in, but one day someone said words that began to frame who she was: “You’re the worst one.” Now admittedly, she says these words could have meant anything, but once she heard them, they hit her and stuck. She thought this meant she was the worst in the family. Now Bishop says she was a very curious, energetic, sometimes mischievous, and aggressive child. She remembers that her siblings usually did not like to horseplay with her because she had so much energy. For example, if they were watching a karate movie the next thing you know she would be flying through the air trying to karate chop someone.

There were three of her siblings that were stair-steppers of which she was the oldest. She was not old enough to go with the older kids, but old enough to babysit the kids younger than her. She began to take on the identity of those words. She talks about leading her brothers and sisters into situations where they would get in trouble. Then she would threaten them and say, “I don’t care if you tell on me because mom is going to leave me with you tomorrow and it will be ten time worse for you than today.” Bishop Ilinda says she would get a spanking everyday reaffirming the fact that she was indeed the worst one.

She started to be tormented in her dreams with nightmares where she was always running and being chased by something dark. She talks about how she began to slip deeper and deeper into this place of darkness. She did not feel like she was worth anything nor did she think she belonged. Her sisters were the picture of beauty, and she just did not measure up. By this point she had no self-esteem. She lived to attack first; she wanted to get you before you even had the chance to do anything to her. Bishop talked about how she could smell fear in people and how she would use that to terrorize them, exploiting it as a weakness. As she became a teenager and boys began to be a part of the equation, this seemed to amplify. She remembers jumping from a two-story window in an apartment complex. In her mind she jumped because she did not care what happened to her. She was numb to everything at this point. All she walked away with was a sprained ankle.

Day 1

Day 2

By this point she started smoking and drinking to numb any pain she was feeling. She believed she was the worst and because she was the worst, she deserved everything she got. Her identify crisis was huge. *For as he* ***thinketh*** *in his heart,* ***so is he (Proverbs 23:7 KJV).*** Bishop Ilinda had taken on the identity of being the worst one; she really believed that in her heart. As a result, she had no idea who she was or where she was going. She had no ambitions, nothing to look forward to. When she became an adult, and went through a divorce, she thought it was her punishment for everything bad she'd ever done. Bishop said it this way: "If you believe wrong you end up wrong. I believed the wrong information that came from the right person." We need to learn how not to be entangled by who people say we are. Our need to be wanted and validated can lead us to places that we have no place going as we search for something that we will never find. I remember when I thought God hated me. Unlike Bishop Ilinda I was raised in the church and taught at an early age who God was. I grew up as a preacher's kid. I knew all the right things to say, but I did not know God. I questioned why I should try to do the right thing--God was sitting in the sky waiting for me to mess up anyway. I was never going to be good enough to be accepted by him. The pressure to be perfect was real in my life; I thought God wanted perfection from me. All I saw was some cruel task master in the clouds that I would never be able to please. I did everything I could to feel wanted and accepted, not really knowing at the time this is what I was looking for. I grew up in a family of all girls. I had a normal childhood with both parents in my home. I was a mama's baby; my twin sister was a daddy's baby. I cannot remember where this thought came from, but as a child I think this Is what framed my thought of God not liking me. I knew my father loved me, but I did not think he liked me very much. In fact, it was not until I became an adult that my view started to change on the matter. It is easy to see why I would have this thought about God since we referr to him as a father. My misguided experience fed me a lie that I perpetuated over and over again. Truth of the matter is, my father was a wonderful man, caring, strong, our protector, and there was nothing he wouldn't do for me.

Day 2

Day 3

I remember Bishop telling us a story of when she was little. There was a church not far from her house and she would sometimes go because there was an older lady there that was nice to her. She would go back just to see if that lady would still be nice to her. Sometimes we have this view of God, and we test him to see if he really loves us, as if he would take his love away. The problem is, like Bishop Ilinda, we have believed the lie in our heart and it has manifested real fruit that we don't understand how to deal with. The truth is you are fearfully and wonderfully made.

When Bishop began to develop a relationship with God, she noticed these places that were broken within her. The process of her conversion started peeling back of layers of hurt, healing the scars and wounds. She loved being in church because it was the first time that she felt as if she belonged. What she did next is as simple as taking your next breath: she believed God. There was no secret formula that washed everything away. She talks about how she read the Bible and it said to pray in your closet. So, she literally thought she was supposed to get in her closet and pray and that is exactly what she did. The presence of God met her right where she was. The more and more time she spent in the closet, the deeper the place of intimacy between her and God became. She began to understand how to navigate her feelings and emotions. She talks about even in the beginning, she still did not think God wanted to use her. However, what she was building in that closet could not be hidden forever. It was here for the first time God revealed his love for her. He revealed identity and acceptance as well. Bishop says real prayer created a real expression of love. By this time, she was behind the curve on a lot of firsts in her life. She said God redeemed the time very quickly. Where she had had no dreams and ambition, she started hitting accelerated milestones in her life. God did what she could not do in a moment and all she did was stand still. Where there was a delay of her blossoming in her career and life God redeemed it in a moment. Suddenly she was working in the prison as a Chaplain for a job that on paper she was not qualified for. After this she went on to get degree after degree.

Joel 2:25 says ***25*** *And I will restore to you the years that the locust hath eaten, the cankerworm, and the caterpillar, and the palmerworm, my great army which I sent among you.* This is a promise that it is never too late. God has a way of allowing time to stand still and accelerate everything you need. True identity is discovered so don't be caught up with what others say or think about you. Bishop Ilinda says her life has been changed a thousand times over each time God reveals another level of her true identity. What that says to me is she is still discovering who he says she is. It is a progressive work. God is wanting to reveal who he says you are. Bishop says she had nothing to offer God, so if he could take her nothing and do something with it, she was going all the way and giving her whole self to the Lord. So, she started with a simple cry of "Yes, Lord," not even looking for a title. As she stepped in this place of humility, she learned how to serve the Lord and love him. She learned how to access the kingdom. Without a shadow of a doubt humility is one of the greatest lessons I have learn from my Bishop. Learn how to stay in this place of discovery with God. As a Christian it is taboo to talk about depression, loneliness, or not having joy or peace. Like I said earlier transparency is one of the things we lack. If I had never been able to see certain sides of Bishop, I think I might still be stuck in a pattern of striving for perfection. She is not afraid to say she's wrong or apologize. She quickly lets go of offense. These are not things that she has told me about herself. They are what I have seen along the way. I have seen people assassinate and challenge her character and integrity and yet she still responds with the love of God. She has learned the art of casting her crowns before the Lord. Every area of advancement in her career and ministry has come to her; she's never had to chase after it. Matthew 6:33 says: *Seek first the kingdom of God and his righteousness and all things shall be added to you.* That is exactly what she did alone in that closet. God became tangible and real to her. What lies have you believed? What label have you accepted? Come to the closet and allow God to give you another revelation that will reveal who he says that you are. Let his never-failing love wash over you and move you from glory to glory as he establishes what his word says about you. Today she is the founder of Raising the Standard Ministry, A network of transitional homes for women and children. Was the president of CMCA (Correctional Ministries and Chaplains Association), Works as a chaplain for D.O.C., a licensed counselor sits as a Bishop over several churches, Senior pastor of The Secret Place Community Church. Just to name a few things that she has had the privilege to accomplish for the Kingdom of God. This was a woman with no hope, no ambition, no self-worth. The worst of the worst whom God has used to do mighty things for his kingdom all because she said yes.

Day 3

Rae

Day 1

I could not think of a better message than this to share with you. My friend Rae has captured the simplicity of receiving God's love in her life. Through a place of heartache and pain she turned her back on God. She was angry at him and blamed him for the hurt and pain she was going through. One of the things I think is important in life to help us navigate through and be reaffirmed (even when it hard to trust anyone else let alone God), is community, which could consist of one or multiple people. Rae's story is so beautiful. How the father pursed her even through her pain is amazing. He used where she was and the community that was around her to help heal and speak his truth to her even while she was believing the lies that she kept telling herself. Her community did not try to change her mind. Instead, they accepted where she was. All the while God never stopped pursuing her heart. I want to share with you something she blogged about in her own words. Her story touched me so much.

Written 07/04/2017

One year ago, I was in a very broken place emotionally and spiritually. You see, I had not spoken to God in over a year. I was angry with Him. My marriage had fallen apart and I wanted Him to fix it. He had not. I was lost, angry, depressed, and in almost total darkness. I could not see anything good about me or that I would ever be happy again. I felt as though I had completely lost myself. My mind could not accept kind words or even begin to believe there would be a future for me. I wanted to believe again...in something...in me...to find happiness or to even begin to like myself again, but I didn't know how.

Most days it was all I could do to get out of bed and go to work. My heart felt completely, utterly, physically broken. I did not understand what it meant to have a broken heart until then, even though I would have sworn I did. I hurt so badly that I literally felt my heart physically break and I was left with a big, gaping, open and hurting void in my being which I was unable and, unbeknownst to me, incapable of even beginning to fill or beginning to mend on my own. Believe me, I tried.

While I was not able to mend my brokenness and I refused to talk to God, He surrounded me with people who I had no clue I needed. After all, I was an island, and I didn't need anyone...I could do it on my own. (If you sense a hint of sarcasm, you are right.) In the meantime, I had a loving boss whom I could call and say "I just can't adult today. I hurt, my eyes are swollen from crying, I couldn't sleep last night and I need to go back to bed." My kind and loving boss would say 'You do such a great job and sometimes you just need to take care of yourself. Get some rest and we will see you tomorrow. I love you!" The wonderful thing about her is that she truly meant it. Words could never express my love for her as well. To this day she is more than a boss, she is a treasured friend.

At the same time, God gave me two beautiful friends whom I have come to realize are my earthly angels. You see, He sent them to me because He knew I would not listen to Him and that's just how much He loves me. There were many times that I would talk with these two wonderful women, and they would impart to me a nugget of wisdom and love that reached my soul in a way that I cannot explain to this day except to say they were God's tools. They would fill me with kind words even when I would not or could not believe them. Statements like "You're not crazy!" "What you are feeling is normal." "You are capable of more than you think." "I have faith in you." "You are strong, smart, loving, kind, generous and you have the wherewithal." "Just look at what you do every day. You're like Superwoman!" "God loves you and He can handle your anger." "You don't have to be healed or perfect to come to God. You come and He will heal you and help you through it." And one statement so very powerful that my world stopped for a moment, and I felt an immediate understanding and connection in my soul with my heart: "God does not think of you the way you think He thinks of you." That moment was a tremendous Ah Ha moment! I realized God loves me...ME! He TOTALLY loves ME! Not the me that others see. Not the me that I allow to show. Not the one that pretends to have it together. Not the one with the fake smile on her face attempting to cover the brokenness; the real uncensored, barely holding on, unable to focus, crazy, sad, lost, dark, confused, scared, fragile, sensitive and completely broken ME!

This was a moment I would never forget. One that carried more weight than most other moments in my life...one that I still remember as vividly as if it happened yesterday. It was a moment that God used to speak to me through the void of darkness deep within me, and my soul responded! I thought on this statement for a while and the way my heart had responded. I did not immediately speak with Him. I had to gnaw on it for a while and roll it over in my mind and heart. I was still angry with Him even though I knew it was not Him I was really angry with.

I still wasn't sure I wanted to talk to Him. In fact, there were times I would feel Him and I would say out loud "I am not talking to you!" Or when someone would mention Him and I would say "I'm not talking to Him. We are not friends right now." In the meantime, I continued in darkness and I had no peace or happiness. I couldn't sleep and I felt lonely and lost all the time. I would say "I can't find me. I'm just so lost and broken. I don't know what to do."

One evening I dropped my two beautiful boys off with their father for the week. Without them I truly felt empty and purposeless. I began driving back to where I lived and sadness and emptiness filled me and I was just so tired. I was tired of being angry and hurt. I was tired of not having peace. I was tired of being lost, empty and broken! I cried out with all my heart and soul; loud, openly, earnestly and needing peace and rest and more than I even knew. I said "God! I am so sad and so so so broken! I am so broken! I can't find peace. I can't find me! I don't know what to do! I can't do this on my own. I need you, please God! Help me! Please! Please help me! I am so sorry! Please help me!" And I sobbed uncontrollably, loudly and with my whole heart. In that moment I was physically driving, but spiritually I was down on my face to God... repenting and asking my Father for His comfort and healing.

In a matter of seconds, I felt peace wash over me, like a literal breath from God. It was just that quick, and I felt the veil of darkness lift from me! I could breathe again and I could feel God again! It was amazing! It was more than I could have ever imagined or asked for. Then my tears of brokenness began to change to tears of thankfulness, relief, love, peace, belief, trust, healing and feelings of calmness and rest in Christ that I don't think I can explain. I had been in darkness and had agreed with depression, sadness, loneliness, and complete brokenness that the devil sold me for so long that I had forgotten the love of Christ! The sheer undeserved and completely humanly unexplainable and totally irreplaceable and unique love of Christ! At that moment I knew beyond everything that God loved me and that He was with me. I knew I would never trade anything for His Peace and love ever again.

I am reminded of a scripture...

"For I know the plans I have for you," declares the Lord, "plans to prosper you and not to harm you, plans to give you hope and a future. 12 Then you will call on me and come and pray to me, and I will listen to you. 13 You will seek me and find me when you seek me with all your heart. 14 I will be found by you," declares the Lord, "and will bring you back from captivity."

Jeremiah 29:11-14

This moment was my turning point. This was when I made a decision to trust God and to follow Him. I sought Him with all my heart and He met me right where I was...broken and lost. He gave me His peace and comforted me when I had no right to ask Him to do so. Of course, He knew that already. In fact, He knew every good thing and bad thing that I would ever do in my life and He sought me anyway. He showed me mercy and love anyway. He forgave me and welcomed me back with open and loving arms. I did not have to clean up first or stop smoking or be a better person. I did not have to make any changes first...He came to me and brought me closer to Him, forgave of all my wrongdoings and helped me to look and act more like Him. It didn't happen overnight, and I am certain He knew it would not.

Now, it is over a year later. I have been recording my journey with God and it is time to share what He has been doing for me. I call these "Love Stories from Jesus" because only He could have written them and only He loves me enough to spend so much time unbreaking me and shining me like a precious gem! Thank you, Jesus, for your unending love! Please use me as your vessel. Everything I am is because of you and I am yours always.!

Love always! Your Unbroken Gem

Have there been times in life where you felt God did not show up when you needed him? Or he was silent when you needed him to speak? What I love about Rae's honesty is she says that she was mad at God and turned to this place of bitterness and darkness that she allowed to grow in her. In this pit God never stopped pursuing her. As her friend told her, God can handle you being mad at him. Most often we do not understand that what we go through can bring about purpose and passion in our lives. Pain is a part of growth; it is one of the beautiful things that works together for our good. Sometimes we do not get the end result that we have hoped for, just like in Rae's story, but it doesn't change who you are or what you mean to God. His love wants to consume everything in your world that is broken and missing. One more point I would like to reiterate is that community was a saving grace for Rae. When she could not stand on her own, she had an Aaron and Hur by her side, holding up her hands, praying and speaking truth to her. They did not make her mask her pain but allowed her to express her feelings while they continued to affirm the truth. I believe this is a huge area of lack in the body of Christ. We do not know how to be each other's community. We spend so much time trying to be like each other. We compare ourselves to one another, not really understanding that everyone's expression is valid and needed. See, what you can't do I can do, and what I can't do you have the grace for. Sometimes I need my inner circle to carry me when I cannot walk by myself. We hold each other up in good times and bad. If I did not have my community through these last two years, I am not sure where I would be. We must learn how to be all things for each other and how to press past this merit system of love to unconditional love. We as the church must understand that we are the answer that men and women are seeking. I pray that we start to move out of this place of surface level relationship to real community that the Bible takes about in the book of Acts, where there were none in need of anything because it was all taken care of by the community.

Day 1

The Doors

Day 1

This part of the book is probably the hardest for me to put into words, simply because it is my story. I want to introduce my sister Danisha. I call her my little big sister. This lady has mentored me in spiritual matters. I have learned so much from her. I would never be able to tell you what a special jewel she is to humanity. The revelation knowledge that flows through her will propel you to the next realm of glory. We have been on a parallel journey the last two years, not even knowing or understanding what God was doing. What's fascinating to me is we were going through one of the toughest periods that we have ever faced as a family. But amid all that God still had a purpose to deliver something to us.

My story was fairly normal growing up. My twin sister and I were the oldest and we have two younger sisters, Danisha whom I've mentioned, and LaToya. Growing up, my parents gave us everything we wanted. Looking back, if we were ever in financial trouble, we never knew it. I remember asking for a camcorder one year for Christmas. I was really into film at the time. Not knowing what my parents had to go through to grant that wish, I later found out how much of a sacrifice it was. From as early as I can remember I experienced fear. The first time I remember was when I was a little girl in my bed. I thought the devil was going to come through the floor of my room and attack me in my sleep. Somehow, I was introduced to fear at an early age. Danisha remembers being in her crib and seeing things or shadows that frightened her as well. I believe my sister was exposed to or aware of the supernatural at an early age. Everything in life scared her. I remember her getting off the school bus one day and running and screaming in terror as if she were being killed because a butterfly was chasing her. If you asked Danisha or me, we would probably both claim the middle child role. My twin Brandi was the popular one who had all the friends; I unfortunately was the tag along little sister, a loaner if you will, wanting desperately to fit in. Danisha was quiet. She was really unable to verbally express what was going on inside of her with her internal fight. For the most part until we were adults, I did not even realize we were going through the same thing. Even with totally normal circumstances we all fought our own induvial battles of lies and perceptions that grew on the inside of us. I think I told you earlier how I felt about my dad. Since Brandi was a daddy's girl, she thought my mom loved me more than her. As a child I was the one who got more attention from mom because I had some health issues growing up. As I grew, fear matured in my life as well.

I remember when I was twenty years old, I had just gotten in some trouble and had been arrested. I was living a lie; I went to church on Sundays but really had no clue who God was. I was serving in the church because since I could remember that is what I was taught to do. My mom was a minister, dad was a deacon. Uncles were Pastors as well. Problem was I did not know what God wanted from me, nor did I believe he loved me. I thought he wanted to punish me for all the wrong I had done. One day I was alone in my apartment and God said, "All I want is you." He took me back to a memory in childhood. There was a lady in our church who we called Sister Wylene Grant. I remember her being a very intuitive person; her relationship with God was something different that we really didn't have a grid for in the Baptist church. This was the first of two of supernatural things dealing with death that I experienced as a child. Sister Grant told my parents to bring the twins to the hospital she as needed to talk to us. I remember her saying that we were going to go through a time when our character was going to be tested and that the things of God instilled on the inside of us were going to be challenged. She told us to hold on and trust God always because he had a mighty work for our hands to do. Now like I said, in our Baptist world we did not have a grid for this type of ministry. We believed the Apostles and prophets died with the first church. I remember calling my mom and asking her about this vision that the Lord had given me as he told me that all he wanted was me. Confirming that it was real, mom was able to go into greater detail of what happened surrounding the event with Sister Wylene. You see, I was in a place where I was searching, and I wanted to know if God was real or not and what his purpose was for my life. That day he spoke to me I had never heard his voice before. At the end of the day, I realized all he wanted was a relationship. You see, he used Sister Wylene to speak a foundation of prophecy over my life that is continuing to unfold to this day. I believe she was so in tune with the Spirit of God she understood her time here on earth and exactly what her purpose was to impart. That day she knew she was going to die, and as she prayed and prophesied over my sister and me she was passing the mantel that lay on her life to the next generation.

When I was about 12 years old, I had my next experience with death. My grandma had a best friend named Larzet Johnson. Again, I think this woman was light years beyond her time. Her gifting and ability in the Spirit realm was beyond what we even realized at the time. One Sunday she went to the front of the church and she began to make amends with people that she thought she offended if her life. Now that day was the 5th Sunday of the month, and on those Sundays, women got to preach. So that night she was slotted to speak. I noticed she kept saying, "God is giving me a chance to get it right, I don't have long." She stood up and said she only had five minutes left. Five minutes passed as sister Johnson said, "Oh Lord, it's been longer than five minutes" and dropped dead in front of the whole church. Why this event sticks out so much in my mind is this was one of the first times that I realized I was a writer. Without any prompting and maybe as a way to work through my emotions of seeing what happened that Sunday, I wrote my first poem. I called it "The Woman I Once Knew." When I tell you that it was the first time that I can look back and say the Holy Spirit was working through me, it is the truth. The maturity and depth of my words could have only come from him. He revealed to me exactly who sister Johnson was. Both women have had a great impact of my life. They were forerunners of what God was bringing the next generation into. As I look back, I discern these women were completely aware of who they were and what God wanted to do through them, even to the place where they did not fear death.

Day 1

Day 2

March 25th, 2019, is the day that changed my life forever. I was in such a place of deception, depression, guilt, shame. By this point I had been in ministry for about fifteen years. I had devoted my life to the things of God. But I still found myself in this broken place. I felt like a failure in everything that I did. I had been fired from my job of ten years just two years prior. Since that time nothing in my life was stable but I thought I was doing what God wanted me to do. Still, on the inside of me, fear ruled. I was in a pit that I was ashamed to tell anyone one about because of the leadership position I walked in at church. I thought I was supposed to have it all together. This was not God's truth but because I lived in this deception it was my reality. I had no peace and my mind constantly told me that I was worthless. On the morning of March 25th, I remember going to church and it was one of the low days for me. I sat in the middle of worship and the Lord said to me, "Are you ready to be with me?" In that moment all I could feel was this love that was so tangible and consuming it is hard to explain. I knew it was the Lord speaking to me and I knew exactly what his words meant. I felt no pain, guilt, or shame in that moment. So, my answer was, "Yes Lord, all I want to do is be with you." I started to feel bad physically through the rest of the service. I texted one of my friends and told her it was getting hard for me to breathe. For some reason, my sister and I had carpooled together that day for church. I had stayed the night at my parents' house because I didn't want to be at home alone. My sister and friend convinced me to go to the E.R. Normally I would have gone home and slept it off. We got to the emergency room and I am going to allow Danisha to tell her side of this story.

Day 2

Door of Agreement

In Danisha's Words

The last two years I refer to as the dark night of my soul. Three times I stared death in the face. Brenda texted to tell me she really was not feeling well, and I got her to the car with the help of some other people. She kept asking me to take her home. I heard the Lord say, "Take her to OU Medical Center." I didn't want her to be mad at me, but I wanted to obey God at the same time. The whole ride there she kept slipping in and out of consciousness. We got her into the E.R. and they took her to a room where they ran all types of tests. I called my parents and they started off to the hospital. As we were sitting in the room, Brenda began to complain that she was cold yet she was burning up. That is when I noticed a shift in the room. I saw her in the spirit, and she was changing from life to death. It looked like a transfiguration of some sort. It was then I noticed I was looking death in the face. I immediately started to pray. I had no grid for this; I had never seen anything like it or experienced It before. Death was in the room as the doctor walked in and told Brenda she had congestive heart failure. At this point they were not giving her much hope and they began to talk about the difficulties she was having with her heart. By this time, the nurses had been trying unsuccessfully for over an hour to get an IV in her. They asked us to leave the room, and I was worried because I saw my loved one lying there with death surrounding her. While we were in the waiting room, I continued to pray as I was bothered by what I saw in the spirit. Suddenly, the open heaven that I saw before me shut. I began to ask the Lord what was going on. His reply to me was to be quiet. So, even though I saw death surrounding my sister, I knew God had instructed me to be quiet. What seemed like an eternity passed by and then the doctor came out to talk to us. I want to point out that he told us he was a Muslim. He then said, "I know your God is real because for seven minutes she lay on my table dead. Come look what your God has done!" Shortly after that they said Brenda was stable for the time being but that they needed to put stents in because she had some blockage to her heart. Brenda made it through the surgery, and they placed her in the ICU. The doctors did not have much hope of her making it through the night and encouraged us to go home and get some rest. By this time, the waiting room was full of family, church family and friends. Brenda's name was being passed all over the country through relationships that she had in ministry for prayer. When I got home that night, I could not sleep as I was still bothered by what I saw and the fact that the open heaven above me was still shut. So, I headed back to the hospital. By the time I got there my older sister, Brandi, was already waiting in the room. One of the nurses started updating us and said we should really pray because she had never seen anyone bounce back with a heart function this low. At that point she only had a 2% heart function. However, this time when I looked at Brenda, I could still feel the presence of death, but life was surrounding her like a light. Right there Brandi and I prayed, but this time I could sense Brenda's spirit man in agreement with us as we prayed. She started trying to wake up. Every time we declared life over her, she would respond by moving or groaning. Five hours later, early in the morning of March 26th at 7 am, Brenda was responding to the nurse. They had no hope that she would have normal brain function since her brain had been without oxygen for seven minutes. She could not use words to communicate because she had a breathing tube down her throat, but she was making a motion to write, asking for a piece of paper. She seemed frustrated that the nurse could not understand what she was trying to point out. She wrote "What time is it?" I knew right there that God had honored everything we prayed that night. You see, this was the first of three doors that God would have me to walk through dealing with death. I call this my door of agreement. What has been revealed to me about this door shows the error that I was walking in as I legislated the things in the earth that God has given me the authority to do. I understand fully well who I am as a son of God in this earth. I know that I stand over an open heaven, and that is why when I saw that door shut, I had no idea of what I was supposed to do. When God told me to wait, I saw death coming for my sister and all I could think was that I have the authority to declare life over her. What I did not understand is that Brenda had some things within herself that she had to settle. You know the saying 'love is stronger than death.' It is true my love wanted Brenda to stay and continue life her with me. That is why God shut the door over me because my prayers could not supersede her will to live or die. You must understand that the same word that Elohim used to form and create the world rests on the inside of you. I could have spoken to legislate what I wanted, not knowing the question that God had already asked Brenda at the start of the day. Through this situation I started to see that I had taken the working stance in so many situations. I can be called to pray, see a thing with wisdom of God and maybe stand in agreement with someone, but in this circumstance, I could not overrule Brenda's will to live or die.

Day 3

Brenda's Experience

Through this period of walking through the dark night of Danisha's soul, we both stared death in the face three time. We did not understand what each other had experienced through this event until months after it happened. So let me continue and tell you this part of the story. To be clear each door to which we were presented to had a revelation connected to the event that we went through but it didn't all happen in the same order for us. Danisha's first door was agreement while my first door was God's agape love. Agape love was Danisha's last door. The second door was the same for both of us.

That feeling of love and peace had never left me since God had talked to me early that morning and asked me if I wanted to be with him. I felt myself surrounded with this peace and love that was so overwhelming, I can't even describe what I felt. The doctor entered the room and said, "You have congestive heart failure." He proceeded to go down the list of exactly what that meant. Suddenly, the totality of death started to sink in for me. I began to have this feeling of being undone. I knew that I had not accomplished all that God wanted me to do in the earth. I told God that I was not ready but wanted to finish. In that moment my whole life flashed before me, and I could not shake the feeling that I still had more that could be done through my hands and feet for God. I don't' remember the initial heart attack but what I do remember is being surrounded by the medical team as they worked on me. I did not experience being out of my body. However, I could not see anything but darkness. I tried but could not open my eyes. I could only hear what was going on around me. I heard the doctor working on me, cursing as he told me to come back and wake up. I heard the conversation of the nurses as they came in and out of the room in the excitement of trying to resuscitate me. The very next thing I remember is waking up in the ICU and trying to communicate with the nurse as she was telling me what happened. The doctors at this particular hospital were desperately trying to get me into a heart program at a local hospital. They had gone as far as they could to care for me. The same doctor who found himself astounded by what God did on his table reached out to a colleague who accepted me into their heart clinic even though I did not meet the criteria for the program. At this point I still had only 2% heart function. I was alive but the doctors were not very hopeful regarding the quality of life that I was going to have. As I lay in that ICU room for two weeks God began to talk to me about who and what I was. The very first thing he said to me was, "I'm going to rebuild your foundation." One of my dearest friends who lived in Texas felt led to come down the first week. Kisha sat in my room four days straight declaring and praying the word of God over me. God gave her the wisdom of what to do. Another family friend, Mamma J as we call her, stayed up all night praying and tearing down everything in the Spirit that did not line up with what God said about me. My church has some of the most intuitive intercessors that I have ever met. Bishop Ilinda had them praying over every negative report that the doctors gave. These intercessors established what the blueprint of heaven said about me. While lying in that bed everything God said he was establishing was done. Through this time, I still felt God's love consuming me. The internal voice that plagued me was beginning to get softer and softer. I remember one day my parents were in the room and they were talking about a young lady who was next door to me who had experienced a heart attack as well. They had met her husband and family in the waiting room. The lady was just 28 years old and had been in a coma for two weeks due to her heart attack. The Lord told me that she was going to wake up in three days. He told me to pray for her husband. I told my parents that I needed them to go get that man because I was supposed to pray for him. Confused, my parent honored my request and brought the man into my room. I prayed for him and his wife. Then I said, "In three days God says your wife is going to wake up." Right before midnight on the third day God did exactly what he said he would do: she woke up. I did not know that God had promised a similar thing to Brandi--that in three days I would start to recover some of the functions I had lost.

This is what I know for certain: I was in a pit drowning, doing everything that I could just to stay afloat. My life was surrounded by lies and fear that had matured on the inside of me and I had no sense of worth or hope, yet I knew God. I served him, worked for him, and did mighty acts in his name. I truly believe God would have honored whatever decision that I made that day. I was not in a place of condemnation. I felt consumed with his tangible love. I believe it would have been okay with God if I stayed or if I left. He left the choice up to me. Literally I chose life, but spiritually I began to be awakened to my true nature and identity. God used those who were praying for me to bring back right alignment and make the path clear for me to stand in the place of spirit and truth. Their intercession made way for me to see God's truth. Danisha could have prayed and raised me from the dead if she wanted to. I am convinced of that. I believe God shut the heavens above her because it had to be my choice. Over the last two years I have begun to get a fuller revelation of who God says that I am especially through these three events that happened in our lives. Where I was stifled by my own way for years, God has truly rebuilt my foundation.

I am reminded of a book series by Rick Joyner called the *Final Quest Trilogy*. It is a recorded revelation that God gave him over twenty-five years ago. What I remember most about these books is he talked about the great battle and a mountain. In the great battle there was an army which was all out of rank, file, and order. Their armor was either missing or not there at all. Rick saw demons riding on these peoples' backs throwing up and defecating. The people were devouring this as their nourishment. Then he made it to the mountain where he found the first level that I want to call salvation. As he ascended this mountain, he found different levels where people had stopped and camped out on certain biblical truths and revelation. As he ascended, he went through the suffering of Jesus and drinking that bitter cup. He moved from glory to glory with God. I have now read this book six times and each time unpacks another level of revelation for me. I thought the mountain represented the church and its future state. Now I am not so sure. I think this depiction represents humanity. Those who are in the battle represent the world. For those of us who have made it to the mountain, this represents the church, those who know God. Now the truth is, there will always be a way for those who are seeking to get to the mountain; there will even be someone there to help you walk through salvation. What stood out to me is how he ascended the mountain. Through his journey some were comfortable with the level of revelation they had already received. But as he moved up the mountain from glory to glory, some levels of revelation allowed him to accelerate until he got to the top. What I am trying to say is I was stuck just like so many of us are stuck on levels where the enemy's arrows can still reach us on the level of revelation we are on. What we do not understand is there is a more excellent way. There is more to the story; we must keep moving and ascending. The higher we ascend, the greater the revelation of truth that rests on us and the easier the things that have been hanging on will fall away because they cannot remain or function in the realm we have been called to rest in. This is the realm of heavenly places seated next to Jesus. It is the place of endless possibilities and the realm of the I AM. In this place you do not focus on what you are not and what you don't have; you see what God see when he looks at you. No lie can exist in this place. You understand who you are and what you possess. This is the place where we reach our fullness in God. Do I have to make it here in order to serve God and be blessed? Certainly not! There are many who are comfortable where they are on the mountain and that is okay. However, God has given us access through Jesus being the door to ascend the mountain and step behind the veil and walk in heavenly places to see the blueprint of heaven and release it in the earth. Welcome to the I AM.

Day 3

Day 4

The Door of Our Inheritance

A little over six months after the first door, on August 8th, we walked through our second door, our inheritance. I was still going through the process of recovery at this point. One thing that was different is how I felt about death. You see, with death I had a choice to stay or go. My heart attack was inevitable. I was not a good steward of my body. That is what caused my heart attack, not the devil or anything else. I want to be very clear about that. However, God honored me in the valley of death. Since that time my ascension started up that mountain as I left the place where I spent so much of my time camped out. On August 3rd I was invited to a gathering at my friend Donna's house. It was a room full of women of God who I had the privilege of being in a prayer network with. We were at this place of intimate worship when I heard the same voice that spoke to me before say the number eight. In that moment I knew it had to do with my grandmother. For the past few years my grandmother had slipped deeper into dementia. For years, my aunt was her caretaker. When God gave me the number eight my immediate thought was God was telling me in eight days my grandmother was going to die. In that moment that same love and peace that surrounded was amplified around me now. I went home and told Danisha, "I think God told me Grandma is going to die in eight days." Danisha told me she thought it would be sooner than that and she began to tell me about a dream that she had that day.

In the dream, she saw Grandma begin to be transformed into this brilliant glorious light. Everything about her became more beautiful as she was being transfigured. She saw Grandma's mind slip into this heavenly realm. Danisha and I began to pray for revelation; I even reached out to Aunt Sandra and Kallena for insight. On August 8th I said to Kallena that I thought God was saying today and not eight days. Within that week my grandmother had drastically started to decline in her ability to even communicate. On a Monday night before she passed my cousins and I were helping my aunt get her ready for bed and I remember knowing in that moment what God had showed me was true. However, I was in complete peace about what God was showing me.

All I saw surrounding her was perfected love. In her death God showed me how much he honored her life and what she had established for him here. Danisha remembers on the 8th that she had taken the day off from work and was resting at home. Dad had just returned from Grandma's house after being there to help her throughout the day when my aunt called him back to the house. Shortly after that she passed, Danisha remembers God saying, "See, love is not strong enough to hold her here in the earth. She has made her decision." Danisha saw in the Spirit how she moved from death to life. In the following days the Lord showed her how my grandmother's spirit hovered over the region that we were in. She began to become a brilliant firework that celebrated her life and all she poured out. Her whole life spoke as a witness for her in that moment. Danisha felt and suddenly understood the inheritance she had gained. She saw my grandfather there as Grandma passed over. In this moment Danisha said she saw the mantels that they both carried. She understood that all our bloodline from the present and into the future had a right to step in and claim these mantels as a birthright. Danisha saw the beauty in this expression of death. In this place none of their shortcomings mattered or stood out; all she saw was pure love.

It took death for us to really see who my grandmother was, but through death this was the greatest inheritance she could have ever left us. Grandma was the one who really introduced us to God. I can remember spending nights at her house and waking up in the morning to her reading the huge KJV bible and having a cup of coffee. She would make all us grandchildren sit in a circle and read that same bible and pray. On Wednesday night she would load us up in her van and take us to prayer meeting. I remember wanting to be there, as the adults cried out for revival and God's hand. We joined in and prayed as well. No one forced us. Through her example God was made so real and tangible to me. She is the reason why I pray now. Some much of who she was propelled me into the hunger for God that has shifted my life from glory to glory. Through her life she deposited something priceless. She was not perfect, nor did she have to be. She was willing and available for God's use. As God began to reveal this truth about her life to me it was a fragrant offering before him with which he was well pleased.

Day 4

Day 5

The I AM

To be honest, this section has taken me two days to write, mainly because I am still walking in certain levels of healing concerning this door and how personal and intimate the revelation has been for both Danisha and me. I remember after my grandmother's funeral I realized how it affected my dad. I feel sorry for dad because I do not think I am ready to know what it feels like to lose a parent. Like I said before, grandma was the pillar of our family. When I saw the grief in my father's eyes, I had no idea on how to help his pain in that moment. I really looked at my father as invincible. I remember one Christmas we had one of the worst snowstorms in history; it literally shut our city down for a few days. I woke up the morning of Christmas Eve and went to work. I lived maybe thirty minutes away from my parents. Usually, our tradition was to spend Christmas Eve night at my parents' house. By the afternoon, the city had shut down from the amount of snow that had fallen. My sisters and I were scattered across town at our various jobs. It took eight hours, but my dad drove and picked us all up. There were people who I worked with that were stranded for the holiday because they weren't able to navigate the weather. From that day forward I was convinced the man was a superhero; there was absolutely nothing he could not do. For six years I saw my father struggle with sickness in his body. After every scare with death that he had always bounced back. One thing that I really appreciate about my dad is when I was sick he and my mom nursed me back to health. I was unable to walk or care for myself. My family did things that went above and beyond. This was the time that I really got to spend with both of my parents and hear about their childhood and our family heritage. I am forever grateful for this time and I thank God for it because he set it up. I did not know the valley we were about to walk through.

Just one month after my grandmother passed away daddy started to complain about pain in his legs. It got worse and worse to the point he could barely walk. Now like me, dad didn't like the hospitals either. One night he had my mom take him to the E.R. because the pain was just unbearable at this point. We found out that my dad was fighting some sort of infection. Remember I said that we were used to him being in the hospital because of all he had already overcome in his health. At this point in his life, he was in the best shape healthwise he had been in for years. The past couple of years he had regained so much energy and could do activities that he had not been able to before. It was like he was a new man. We never expected that he would not come back home. We were so accustomed to him bouncing back. For two weeks he stays in the hospital fighting this virus. The doctors felt he was strong enough to leave but want him to go to a rehab facility because he had not walked in two weeks. They wanted him to rebuild his stamina. Then they said he would be able to come home and continue with life. This was great news--one more hurdle before he came home. My dad was in great spirits and was back to his normal self. But after about a week of being in the place he started having issues with his kidneys. The facility was not adequately equipped to take care of him.

It was a Friday and my aunts had been with daddy most of the day so my mom could return to work, and when I got there, he was having a hard time breathing. One of the doctors finally decided that he needed to be transferred back to a hospital. By that Sunday my mom and sisters and I were all hanging out, talking to my dad. He seemed to be doing so much better, laughing and making plans for what we wanted to do next as a family. What I have forgotten to mention and really didn't notice until I went through the process was that during this whole month of him going through this sickness, he started doing the same thing that sisters Grant and Johnson did before they died--making sure that there was no offense left between him and anyone. Also, he was depositing what he had in the way of spiritual inheritance and wisdom that he had to pass to the next generation. That Sunday my dad coded, but the power of love that we had for him prayed him back to life, but it was not because he was not ready. We were not ready to let him go for 12 days; he hung on to allow God to prepare us for a decision he had already made. While he was in in the hospital, one day he sang a song by James Fortune called The I AM. He mouthed the words to the song while it played. This was the message he was trying to leave us. In all he ever did for us he always made sure his family was taken care of. During this twelve-day process I remember asking God why this came out the blue and why he did not prepare me for what was happening. With my grandma he told me the day of her death and it was a celebration of the beauty of who she was, but with my dad I felt blindsided. That is when he directed me to a conversation I had with my friend Kisha. I told her I did not care what happened if my dad died, I was going to go right in that room and raise him from the dead because I knew what God could do. He response was not what I wanted to hear at all. She said, "Yes, Brenda, that's true, but what if that's not your dad's choice?" In that moment my love was stronger than death, and in that moment I had forgotten everything that I had walked through, not understanding that the same option that was offered to me by God was now being offered to my father. His answer was the words of a song: *I have all that I need because the great I AM has provided for me.* In that moment, the Lord said, "Well-done, thou good and faithful servant." Everything that daddy had to give he had already imparted and poured out. There is a picture of my dad and grandmother right before she died where she has her hand on his head as if she were praying for him. I wholeheartedly believe that she was anointing him for what he was about to walk through.

Three days before he died my aunt from Houston and I were in his room and he had finally awoken and was able to interact with us. Now this is after my declaration of saying I would raise him from the dead. My dad grabbed my hand, squeezed it, and looking at me, he told me he loved me. He had this intense look and stare in his eyes; he never broke his gaze. He kept saying repeatedly with tears in his eyes, "I love you." It was in that moment that I realized he was telling me goodbye. Two days after that I was at the hospital just waiting in his room. All day he looked at the door, holding a conversation with someone. I thought he was talking to me; I kept asking what he said or if he needed something. He acted as if he were bothered, as though I was rudely interrupting a conversation with someone I could not see. For two days he had this conversation. What I think is he caught a glimpse of something. I want to make room for Danisha to tell you her experience through this door because I know what has been revealed to her is a glimpse of what my dad walked through.

Day 5

Day 6

Danisha's account

On Sunday we were at the hospital. My mom was urging us to come in the room. Once again, I could not shake what I saw in the Spirit. It was the expression of life leaving my father's body. I told God, "If you take him, I'm going in that room to raise him from the dead." Once again, I found myself locked out of the heavens, I was mad at God. I am a daddy's girl for real. My dad worked the graveyard shift and my mom said I would stand in my crib and wait for him to get home from work. She was not able to put me to sleep because I wanted him. He was my hero who taught me what my worth was and what a man should and should not be. I saw him study the word and pray. I saw how strong yet vulnerable he was when it came to his girls. I was not prepared nor ready for him to leave; we were so use to him bouncing back. Oct 19, 2019, what was revealed to me has set me on a trajectory and has forever changed my life. I believe that Brenda mentioned earlier how we walked through the same doors but maybe not at the same time. She experienced the tangible love that was expressed to her through her sickness and my grandmother's death. I got to see God open the heavens and let me peer into a place so glorious that I don't have adequate words to describe it. I want to share what I saw in the realm of the I AM. When dad passed away, I was immediately transported in the Spirit. I saw him standing there, dressed in a burgundy suit looking like a younger version of himself. He was smiling and surrounded by this glorious light. As he ascended, knowing that his soul was leaving the earth, I started quoting Psalm 23. I saw this swirling energy come and combine with this brilliant illuminating light that was surrounding him. I had never seen anything like it and I knew he was being transformed into his glorious body. Suddenly I was being shifted into this portal where I found myself surrounded by unexplainable love which was so tangible, so thick, so consuming, so overwhelming. The more I gave myself to this place I started to hear all these voices crying out in different languages and dialects. I started to know and recall names of people who passed through this place. I automatically had answers of wisdom, knowledge and revelation for things that have plagued humanity. I knew the answer. It was like I was standing in the middle of God's information highway.

I heard all of humanity from different religious backgrounds all calling out to God in prayer and supplication. It was here that I found the mystery of how all things work together. Here is where I saw all things that connected all of humanity, with earth and creation all streaming and ascending through this place surrounded by this unmeasurable love. In this place all things worked in perfect harmony. I remember thinking, "God, how did I get here and what is this?" Suddenly I knew I was standing in the realm of the I AM. I saw my dad ascending and being surrounded by this love. I saw him being transfigured into this luminous light. This is the place where I met Father God. Over the next few days, I was stuck in this place of revelation. I felt my father's spirit saturating us and watching over us as we navigated our new reality. I remember that I did not really grieve during this time. It was not until the casket shut for the final time on my dad that I heard him say in the Spirit, "It was imperative that I left; if I never did you would never accomplish your assignment." I began to weep uncontrollably because I knew exactly the weight of what he meant. Though this door of the death of my dad the I AM was revealed to me. Suddenly, in one moment, I had answers and revelations to things that God wanted me to unlock and bring into the realm of humanity. I understood mysteries and secrets of the kingdom. The key to all these things was surrounded by this expression of love that Brenda had talked about, which was made so real and tangible to me. I understood that this was the thing that gave me access to live in the fulness of who God had called me to be. Suddenly things that were important to me did not matter anymore. This experience has catapulted me into the next. No matter how many times I have closed my eyes since then, I still find myself in this place of love. I can't deny it nor shall I ever forget what has been revealed to me. Each day the Lord continues to unpack the fulness of it, giving me wisdom and strategy of how to release and share it here.

Day 6

Day 7

What God reveled to Danisha is so powerful I am convinced that we are entering a new dispensation in time, a new era, if you will. The age of the Sons of God. Just as I shared previously about the mountain, it is okay if you choose to stay where you are, but the fact remains we have been given access. Access to ascend into the realm of the I AM and download the blueprint of heaven to be released here on earth. This love flows to and through humanity; there is no separation to God. We have bought into this idea of a merited love system. We say with our words that our love is unconditional and quote scripture like Corinthians 13 (Love keeps no record of wrong), but our love only keeps a record of love. It shows by the fruit that we bear, what we try to build in the name of the Lord, but mostly how the earth is still waiting for manifested sons. You see, we are not waiting on God. He is waiting on us to realize who we are and what we have in us to be unlocked for his Glory. The time for the one-man show is over, the key to the kingdom is love and unity. They are the only thing that unlocks the door.

[32] And the multitude of them that believed were of one heart and of one soul: neither said any of them that ought of the things which he possessed was his own; but they had all things common.

[33] And with great power gave the apostles witness of the resurrection of the Lord Jesus: and great grace was upon them all.

[34] Neither was there any among them that lacked: for as many as were possessors of lands or houses sold them, and brought the prices of the things that were sold,

[35] And laid them down at the apostles' feet: and distribution was made unto every man according as he had need (Acts 3:32-35 KJV)

This is the blueprint of heaven, the keys to the Kingdom. In this place of oneness and unity there was not one need or concern. This is the place we are being called to as we ascend this mountain. We will gain access to realms and understanding of solutions for our world. However, love and unity are the only way we can live continuously full in this place. I am convinced what Danisha saw was a foretaste of what God is releasing in this hour. The tip of the iceberg. In days to come scripture and words that we have read and had a basic carnal understanding of will become real to us in so many different ways. The Word of God is alive and active, accomplishing what we cannot yet see with our natural eyes. But God is giving those of us who desire vision for what shall be established in the earth, once you see you have the ability to establish it. Just like the Elohim Creator God said in Genesis, "*Let us go make man in our image and likeness*", that's what rests on the inside of you to create what you need in the time that you need it. Align yourself with the knowledge and blueprint of heaven to release the sound that this earth has eagerly been awaiting. These last ten years of my journey have been only a set up to get me to this place. Through the process of writing this book I can physically see how the hand of God orchestrated every event to bring me to this point of freedom. In 2018 I was so done with the church and the things of God; I spoke to my friend Kisha all the time about these things. In the middle of my complaint God began to stir something new within both of us. We came to this place of accountability; we were both on the edge of throwing in the towel. He patiently began to renew and walk us out of this place where we were stuck works and the things we knew about God, but lacking the real presence of God in our lives. We started studying Rees Howell's intercessor book. It really did ignite and start a new fire within us. We always had this saying from the book "I'm going to the train station" which stemmed from an encounter that he and his wife had. They heard the voice of God say "Go" but had no funds in the natural to go anywhere. So, they just showed up at the train station not knowing how they were going to get the resources they need. All they understood was to go.

I had no idea what I was about to walk through in 2019 but Kisha and I were making plans to go to the train station. We can sit back and laugh about it now because we only understood in our carnal mind and thinking what that meant. We made it to that train station; the day of my heart attack my sister remembers that as she left the room, I told her to call Kisha. She says it was really the only lucid thing she remembers me saying. Kisha recalls getting the call and asking God "Why is she calling for me? What do I have, what can I do besides pray?" You must understand that she lives in a different state. At this time, she had just left a corporate job because she heard the voice of the Lord telling her to. She was in the middle of her own life issues. Her husband really did not understand why, or where God was leading her. She said that night she heard God say "Go." She didn't really want to and assumed that her husband's response would be no because they were in a place of financial difficulties from her job decision. She could not sleep until she obeyed. She told her husband that she was to go spend the next week with me. She entered the train station not knowing where she was going to stay, feed herself, or provide what she needed on the way. Before she could get on the road God had provided everything she needed. Kisha knew exactly where I was spiritually because she had walked with me there, she knew my disappointments and fears. God allowed both of us to be transformed at the same time. Everything that I experienced through my transformation from death to life, God was showing her. Remember I told you there was a friend who stayed in my room night and day declaring scripture and the truth of the foundation that God wanted to rebuild? That was Kisha. She prayed, sang, worshiped, and created a tangible atmosphere of God's presence. What is really amazing is that we were seeking God and we both walked through that love and peace together.

> We have overcome by the blood of the lamb; we are not waiting for this fullness; we already walk in it. It is being renewed by the word of our testimony over and over again. Through the next 100 days of this devotional, I want you to really hear the voice of God and find what he is calling out for you. Discover what he wants to bring in access and alignment. I want us to cross over into the realm of the I AM, ascending the mountain to stay in the place of his presence and light as he reveals himself to you in a greater way. This devotional is broken up into two different volumes. The first is called *The Awakening of the Sons of God*; it is meant to reawaken you to original intent and knowing God's truth and love about you. The next is called *What Shall I Manifest?* You will have an opportunity to have a very introspective look into where you are and what you have allowed to manifest as fruit in your life. I am very excited to share and go on this journey with you. Along the way I have provided areas for you to journal exactly what is being revealed. Once again, I want to welcome you to this new era and time. Welcome to the reign of his glory; what shall you manifest?

Day 7

Volume 2

Awakening the Sons of God

This work has taken me over ten years to create. In the summer of 2011, I remember being in awe of how Sarah Young came up with the idea of *Jesus Calling*. She just sat and listened to what God had to say. I thought why not, and truth be told, I really did not have a clear vision of what the voice of God sounded like in my ear. It was filtered with my feelings of condemnation and shame of not being enough, not being what I thought he wanted me to be. The truth is I was desperately needing him to speak, and I was doing all the things I thought he wanted me to do. However, my heart was full of religion and ignorance. Why ten years? I can't really answer that accurately; all I can say is the whole time God has been waiting on me. I thought I was waiting on his hand to move and show me what to do with this work, but the whole time he has been waiting on me to manifest as a maturing son who truly sees him with the right eyes.

Theses entries are somewhat personal yet at the same time I think you can relate. They are written as our father speaking to us. My hope is that you take this journey with me and listen to what he is saying to you. There will be a place for you to respond because I firmly believe when we hear the Lord speak, we should have a response even if it's nothing more than amen. This body of work is separated into three different volumes. "Awakening of the Sons of God", "What Shall I manifest?" and "The Reign of His Glory." I am very excited to share what God has placed on my heart with you in hopes that you find your true identity and encouragement as a Son of God. You are needed to manifest the Kingdom of God right where you are.

Day 1

Where are the Levites?

What are you looking for? Have I not given you everything you need? You are always wanting but never satisfied. You do not know how to tap into what you already have on the inside. I have called you to minister to me, to stand in this earth and release all of me. Where are my Levites? Where have you gone? Why are you sleeping? Arise and hear my voice, arise and see where I am and what I am doing. In this hour you must see beyond what your natural eyes see. I AM is showing you the way. You have everything you need; the power lies within what you speak. Speak wisely, understanding you breathe life into everything you say. Stand firmly where you are. I have called you to minister before me that you might reach out and cover the earth with my love. Hear the clarion call: the time is now that you must stand in your rightful place. No longer can you delay. I AM is moving now, restoring now. Where are you, my Levite?

Day 1

Day 2

The Plumbline

This is an hour of realignment, an hour of reconstruction. Just as God asked Amos in Amos 7:8, "What do you see?", he is asking those who see the same question. For God has dropped a plumbline in the midst of his people that will challenge what you believe and call holy. Let us be very clear: some religious things we hold onto and traditions we hold dear will never survive. We have convoluted the foundation of God with things that were never meant to remain. We have built up systems that have nothing to do with God. In order to move forward a shaking must occur and everything that is unshakeable will remain. Everything that needs to go will no longer be able to stand. When a builder drops a plumbline from the top of a structure he is building, it acts as a tool that keeps everything in alignment so that the structure does not lean too far to the left or right, but stays straight, the way it was designed. In this season allow God to deal with the sacred cows in your life. Follow him to the place he is calling and leading you.

Day 2

Day 3

Meditations of my heart

There is something on the inside of you that the earth and all of creation have been yearning for. I want to unlock the ancient wells that flow deep within you. Can you hear the deep calling? Can you feel me pulling you closer? Closer to my sight where we are face to face. This is the place you were always meant to be. Understand I have created you to live in two places at once. What you see in the natural is not your reality. Ask for eyes to see and ears to hear what the Spirit is doing. For it is there you live and exist. The natural realm is where you are, but at the same time you are a conduit to release my Glory and my kingdom which lives inside you. A Kingdom that has not been made by the hands of man, a kingdom that is full of love and peace. A kingdom of dominion, full of kings and priests. Where are you O King? Where are you O Priest? Stand in the place in which I have called and ordained you to stand. Hear the word of the Lord, shake off your grave clothes, shake off the slumber, and rule! The deep is calling you back in alignment. Rule as my Son here, release my kingdom here, have dominion here. For I have called you out of the grave so keep one hand connected to me and walk this earth.

Day 3

Day 4

Come in

Come in,
Come in,
Come in,
come in and dwell in me.
I am yours forever.
I want to feel your presence surrounding me.
Let your glory flow through me,
Your manifested power work through me.
Come on in.
Consume me with your love.
Let your glory wash over me.
I want to be complete,
Complete in you.

Day 4

Day 5

Drink from My Well

Your thirst has not been satisfied. You search here and there for something you cannot find from the hands of man. What I offer you is something eternal, everlasting, never ending. You have hoped and prayed for something more, crying out to me and asking, "Is this it? Is this all you have to offer me?" Come to my well with expectancy; come to my well with your hunger. For you have an insatiable appetite that only I can fill. You have spent your time consuming things that are only temporary and which lead you to dead ends. They cannot satisfy you. Press past the quick fix and come deeper into my chamber, allowing the root of your heart to go deep. Just like a tree planted by the rivers of life I will supply you with everything you need. My well will never run dry.

Day 5

Day 6

Tower of Babel

Understand the power of the gift I have given to you. The power of the mind. Power in unity. I say to you there is nothing you cannot do. You have the power to manifest what you need. You spend so much time caught up in "magical thinking", waiting on me to move and deliver. But just as I asked Moses, "What do you have in your hands?", I ask you. You have the ability to manifest your reality. I instruct you to think upon things that are lovely and pure. What you release in your sphere of influence is up to you. The question you should ask is, "Am I the master of my mind (my thinking), or is it mastering me?" See, you were created to subdue and rule, not be held captive by your thoughts, some of which manifest fear and unbelief in your life. These thoughts are the path that will suppress your true identity. Just like the children of Babel--there was nothing they could not accomplish--they were of one heart and one mind. My problem with them was their heart and mind did not line up with my will. They had their own selfish ambitions, and agendas. Even today the curse still stands to those who have not found how to tap into the language of unity. When you hear the heartbeat of the kingdom language you cannot comprehend it. I understand this message is not for everyone. Only those with ears to hear, hear what the Lord is saying and draw near.

Day 6

Day 7

The New Era

Are you ready? Here I am, standing at the door knock, knock, knocking. It is you who I seek, whom I pursue. You are light, the light of this world shining so bright that you reflect my glory. I am ushering in a New Era; have you not perceived it? It is the time when the Sons of God will walk in majesty. The earth and creation have long waited for the day of the kingdom. The dispensation of time has faded from the age of the church. Now you stand boldly in the place of the kingdom which Is being made manifest all around you. See with your eyes and with your heart and understand that nothing is impossible. I have preserved you for this day. This hour is your time. Cover the earth with my glory, cover the earth with my explosive power. King, priest, son, can you see yourself ruling in the place I have called you to live? The air is different here with possibilities unending. Bring forth my kingdom. Now is the time of unity, so minister to the widows, orphans, those who have no peace, those who need to be found. Release, release o ancient wells the river of life that invites all who are thirsty to drink. The days of your war are over; no longer will you fight for what has already been freely given to you. I invite you to be the place of Bethel, the place where I live.

Day 7

Day 8

Prophecy of the Tree
Psalm 1

And he shall be like a tree planted by the rivers of water and shall bring forth his fruit in due season. His leaves shall not wither and whatsoever he does shall prosper.

I am waiting for you to take root and be grounded in me. You have begun to sprout and yet there is no depth found in you. The reason you find yourself in doubt is because have failed to search out the water that can sustain you. It may quench your thirst for a period, but you still walk away depleted. In this weak state you try to fight, but allow me to prophesy to the tree. Prune out the dead nature and bring back to life all that I have planted in you. Do not be afraid to go deep and explore my dimensions and see my glory. Grab hold and anchor yourself deep within my river. Allow my waters to overtake you as I keep you grounded.

Day 8

Day 9

What He Wants to Get Out
John 14:16

And I will pray to the Father, and he shall give you another comforter, that he may abide with you forever.

He is wise and only moves if I say so. He is from the beginning of time, an ancient Spirit. He works better when he is allowed to move within, upon, and through you. He is a teacher; he has wisdom that transcends that which has or will ever walk upon the face of this earth. Who is he? My comforter, teacher, voice, my Spirit. I am he, and he is me. We are one. Accept him and he will show you marvelous things. Surrender to him, giving me full control. Call for him and out of the depths of you he will awaken you to new realms of possibility. He will usher you into the place I have ordained for you to walk. He lives inside you.

Day 9

Day 10

Abide in Me
John15:4

Abide in me and I in you; the branch cannot bear fruit of itself, except you abide in me.

Come, come, I have prepared a table before you. You say you are hungry, but I have freely given you my body for bread and my blood. If you would only partake, sit at my table, and taste and see the wonderful delicacies I have prepared for you. If you sit with me you are qualified to rule with me. Oh, how I love you; I have waited and longed for you. It saddens me when you do not trust me. I have chosen you; I have adorned you to walk with me. You are the reflector of my beauty and majesty. Seek me to validate you for I am the only one who can. Learn of me the ways of joy, peace, and love, long suffering, gentleness, meekness, and patience. Come to the table and learn of my wisdom. I will never give up on you; I will always pursue intimate relationship with you, my love, my joy.

Day 10

Day 11

Leaking

Remember the joy you felt that day you gave your life to me. You surrendered and came home, and a great shout erupted in heaven over the news. My joy could not be contained. I wept at your decision to choose me. My child, be aware there is an enemy lurking in the shadows. His ways are subtle and sometimes hard to detect. He is very patient in order to get what he wants. His attacks are sometime like the prick of a pin which create a slow leak. Compromise is his weapon of choice. He cares little about how much you go to church. His ultimate agenda is to stunt your growth, to get you in a place where you say "Lord, didn't I do this in your name? I served and accomplished mighty victories in your name!" But your heart is far from me. The enemy's game is simple: he will confuse your mission with church work so that you are busy serving, but the whole time you are leaking. The you come to the ended of yourself feeling unfilled in me. You are leaking, not refilling, leaking and not refilling. This makes his job easy, for now you are too tired to seek my face. You can no longer understand my will. You start to be lulled to sleep by his whisper and your despair. You have too much going on to fit me in and you misinterpret my message of love to what fits your agenda and purpose. All the while you are leaking and not refilling. Can you hear me calling you? He wants to separate you from me and sever the connection that flows between us. Come drink of me, eat with me. Seek me now while I can be found. Come away and just be with me, my child. I will teach you how to make your armor fit and protect you from his prick.

Day 11

Day 12

Ignite Me
Hebrews 12:29
Our God is a consuming fire

Began to stir the fire of your heart. Many of you ask for my fire and have no idea what to do once you have it. Just like kindling helps ignite the flame, there is always something there that feeds it. Let me start with the loose bushes and shrubs in your life, clearing the way to birth something new. I want to consume you; let us not stop there. I want to burn that flesh that leads you to bondage. Ask me to set you ablaze so that everything you touch is consumed. I want you ignited and burning with my fire. I will burn upon and within you, never destroying you. It is there we shall commune together becoming one. A beautiful light spreading across this land. This fire that burns within you makes way for my kingdom to rest here. Ask me to be ignited, to be consumed. For I shall come swiftly!

Day 12

Day 13

Go Behind the Veil
Isaiah 61:1

I have placed my Spirit within you. You have been anointed to tell of the good news of my kingdom. You have the authority to heal the broken hearted, to bring to liberty those who are found as prisoners. So many of my children are living just to die and go to heaven. I have called you to a place of purpose and given you passion to be released in this earth. Salvation is not the end but rather the beginning of the story. To enter my kingdom, press past the outer court. Go beyond the brazen altar. I want to meet you beyond the veil face to face. For it is in this place that I shall reveal my secrets and mysteries. There is a world that is dying; the people do not know my love, joy, peace, or freedom. They need the answer, the key. You are that answer and key they seek. I have so much more in store for you; greater works are in your mouth. When you establish my kingdom, darkness is broken giving way to the light.

Day 13

Day 14

The Blood Still Speaks
Hebrews 9:12, Mark 14:24

The Blood of Jesus is precious. By it I have covered everything that was and is to come in your life and opened every door available to you, while shutting those that lead you away from me. The power of the blood has destroyed all sickness and disease, resurrecting and restoring you to my original design. The power of the blood has rescued you to me. So why have you made it worthless? "How is that?", you say. It is when you murmur and complain, allow weariness in well doing and when you fail to see your path as temporal and not your true reality. It is when you lose sight of me in the middle of the storm. I hear the blood crying out, wanting to work in all areas of your life. Wanting to comfort and release you from every false burden you have collected as your own. Change your mindset for the blood has given you everything you need to live abundantly. This storm is not your reality; I AM is your reality. Allow stinking thinking to be cast down and step into the realm of my glory for we shall move together to heights and depts that you have never seen.

Day 14

Day 15

Ichabod
1 Samuel 4:21

There is a cost to have my Glory. You must learn how to possess it for many have fought after, misrepresented, and prostituted themselves for it. In their ignorance they have led many astray to a place of bondage and fear. I want to dwell with you in the secret place where I can cultivate my nature in you. You say you want me and cannot live without me; however, your heart is far from me. Watch your motives and bring them to my fire so they might be purified. For I smell the fragrance of your worship before me, and it is not always pleasing. I want to take control; however, I need you to surrender. What shall become of my bride? Her pride has driven me away. Oh, how I long to draw near and embrace her once again. Repent and come quickly back to me, your first love. There I will endow you with my fire, my power. For the curse of Ichabod shall be destroyed; no longer will it have its work in your life. Men and women will tell of my Glory through your hands.

Day 15

Day 16

Kill the Queen
Revelation 18:4

Awaken, my child, for your slumber has been too long. Now is the time you must choose whose side you are on. I have watched you linger between two opinions for far too long. One minute I have the throne of your heart, next it belongs to the systems of this world. Come out of her for you must destroy this queen who has erected her throne right in the midst of your heart. Shake yourself loose from those systems that have lulled you to sleep. Awake to my unconditional love, for this is the most powerful weapon you possess. You must use it to kill the queen. Her time has come, her throne must fall. Who is this queen? Any system created that is void of my love, joy, peace, grace and mercy, and anything that keeps you ignorant of your true identity and the power the lies inside you. I have created a way out, a way of escape for you. The systems of this world no longer hold any power over you. Release yourself from this false imprisonment now so abundant life may rest upon you. Come out and stand guarded with the helmet of salvation, belt of truth, breastplate of righteousness, and move with the gospel of peace.

Day 16

Day 17

The Enemy Within
Hebrews 13:1

Be careful to do everything in love. Correct in love, teach in love, serve in love. How is it that love does not abide much more in you? What I find among you is bickering, competition, selfish ambition. Those things only serve you and no one else. I have given you inherited wealth that cannot be measured. Seek my kingdom and you will open the door. You have become an enemy within the gates, bearing my name only and not my heart. No fruit has been found to testify of my Glory. If you let me, I will show you a more excellent way. Let my Spirit walk you into all truth, lay yourself on my altar and become an instrument for my use. I will teach you how to wear my mantle of humility and walk in every gift I have given you.

Day 17

Day 18

Battlefield
2 Corinthians 10:5

It would do you good to listen. Many of you fail simply because you never challenge your imagination. Every thought you think is not yours alone, for spirits and principalities have come to wage war on this battlefield. They will infiltrate your thinking, giving you a false idea of who is really on your side. As a man thinketh so is he. The enemy cannot read your mind although he can suggest thoughts that you take on as your own. Then you bear fruit that grows from his implanted thoughts combined with what comes out of your mouth. You must understand: your mind is a power weapon in your arsenal, and it does bear fruit. So which fruit will you bear? Out of your mouth I have given the power of life and death, blessings and curses. It is on this battlefield seeds are planted and eventually a harvest will come. Everything that exalts itself against my knowledge, nature, word, and love must be cut down and thrown into the fire. You possess the mind of Christ; no longer will you be overtaken by lies that come as messengers of light. Try each spirit by the Spirit for this will expose everything that can't stand in the light.

Day 18

Day 19

Who Has Your Heart?
Song of Solomon 2:10

My beloved, my heart is turned toward you and only you. Do you know you affect me in ways you will probably never realize? You could search all eternity long to find the width and depth of my love, but you would never find it. My love toward you is immeasurable and without end, for you have my heart. I have willingly given you all of me holding nothing back. No boundaries, no walls separate me from you. In every way possible I have called you to come and be one with me. I have watched you lend yourselves out to others who are not worthy of you. I have watched you prostitute yourself in search of what only I can give. Hear my words and take heed; allow me to remove all shame and guilt from you. Come unto me for I have conquered all. I am for you. If you only knew how deeply my love burns for you. I am driven by my passion toward you, and I will purify you. I will be your covering. I have hewed you out of stone into a thing of beauty. I have placed myself within you making us one; we are married to one another. You have my heart. I am my beloved's, and my beloved is mine.

Day 19

Day 20

I Am Not Dead

I came, died, and rose again. I am not dead. I walked this earth in denial of my flesh, as a man. All power had not been given to me yet. I am not dead. I walked and toiled in my wilderness for 40 days, not to be overtaken by the enemy within. Power was then endowed upon and within me to do great and mighty works. Along with the Spirit I worked while it was day. Behold, when night comes no man can work. I willingly chose Calvary to insure you have a way to be reconciled back to Father God and your true identity in me so that you will not live as orphans any longer. For you shall do greater works; I am the gate which you walk through. You will receive truth and life through me. Come and stand in the place of I AM because here you can release a kingdom that has not been made by the hands of man. I will be your hands, feet, mouth, heart upon this earth. I am alive in you, and you must bring our Father's Glory.

Day 20

Day 21

Be Still
Psalms 4:10

My child, be anxious for nothing but rest on the fact that I am your source. Take your time to get still and quiet before me; it is here we shall commune. I will give you the strategy and the answers you seek. You can trust my voice so cast everything on me and allow me to lead you into all understanding. In exchange I will give you my joy and peace. My arm is never too short to provide everything you need. There is no room at my table for worry or doubt. Be still and know I am your provider who works on your behalf.

Day 21

Day 22

In the Middle of the Night
1 Thessalonians 5:18

Sometimes you stay in a place of night and despair because of the fruit of your lips. Day comes and you are cast down by the words you speak. Do you not know your tongue is an active, living, breathing part of your body, delivering whatever fruit has been found in the pitfalls of your mind? You should never despair of this place called midnight for you have the power to overcome it. Stop confusing a season for your reality. Seasons are meant to carry you to the next realm of Glory in me. They are an activation to unlock yet another secret that holds your true identify. Go through the process and keep moving. Do not stand still too long. I will train you in the art of war, teaching you how to live in and out of season. I am equipping you with night vision so that you may take the spoils of any enemy lurking to devour you.

Day 22

Day 23

How to Walk

You know me by the Spirit. You know my truth and must have faith in my truth. Trust that it is my hand moving and working through you. My voice speaks through you, my heart speaks through you. Keep moving, do not give up, do not slow down, but keep pace with me. Chase hard after me. Be steady with my Spirit for you surely shall not faint.

Day 23

Day 24

Restore the Temple
2 Corinthians 5:17-19

I want to restore my temple that dwells inside you. All that lies in ruins I will rebuild. You are my dwelling place. All that has died and gone dormant within in you I will bring to a place of new life. You have come to me broken and empty; I will fill you with wonders of my Glory. I will manifest my power through you to demonstrate exactly who I am. Your desire is to see me move; I will do it through you. This temple I am restoring eyes have not seen before. Meditate on me day and night and allow my eternal flame to consume your very nature. It is I, your God, who will do a new thing.

Day 24

Day 25

I AM is Here
Luke 5:18-19

Push past all the obstacles, excuses, problems, and situations. Push past everything that clouds your view of who I am. Do not give up. Why are you taking no for an answer? Keep moving until you can identify the door I have for you. I AM is here walking beside you; just step in sync with where you see me leading. My child, I have never left you alone, so reach out and grab my mighty right hand which is strong enough to hold you. Take hold of me and lose the grip on the things you can no longer hold. I will never let you go.

Day 25

Day 26

I Am Willing
Luke 5:13

I am willing and have always been willing for you to come to me. In fact, the blood of Jesus has made way for you to come to me. Death, Hell, and the grave must now obey you. Diseases, sickness, and infirmity now fall under your feet. You have triumphed over it all. What shall you say then to these things? Every debt that you would ever face has been paid in full. You owe no penalty. You are free for I was willing to take all your debt for you. Now you can experience what abundant life really should be. So, my question to you is: Are you willing to receive my gift of freedom?

Day 26

Day 27

Love
1 John 3:14-16

I have commanded you to love one another. Even now it is hard to find my agape love in the earth. You love comes with conditions and standards that only serve you. I have called you out of darkness to a place of illuminating light. You say you belong to me, yet you don't look like me. Ask me and I will give you the temperance to walk in the ways of unconditional love, a love that does not seek to fulfill its own lustful desires. Consider the power of your response when it is found deeply rooted in me. Fall in love with me so that you may fall in love with my children. I have given you a perfected love that casts out all fear and shame. The only key to activate my kingdom and heal your world is to be grounded in love. I invite you to travel the corridors of my heart that you may know this love.

Day 27

Day 28

Get Closer
Ephesians 6:12

You war is not waged in the fleshly earth realm. Come closer and ascend to my mountain. Here you will see the enemy's attacks before they come. Ascend even higher and take your seat at my right hand. I have called you my King, Priest, and Son. I have given you majesty that cannot be tried or tested and found you righteous and worthy in Christ. Come be seated with me that you may rule with dominion and power.

Day 28

Day 29

Mortify the Flesh
Romans 8:13

If you live by the flesh, you shall surely die by the flesh. If you live by the Spirit, it is here you are choosing life. You must mortify and annihilate your flesh, for in it is found no good thing. Place you mind on higher things, thereby creating an opportunity to manifest good that flows from your hands. My Spirit calls out to the deep wells within you and calls for the waters to rise so that the overflow will spill out to the nations. The works of your flesh stop the flow of my kingdom. I have given you the ability to rule your flesh so that it will not rule you. Come to grips with the nature of the seeds you have planted, and no longer let the fruit of deceit work in you. Allow my Spirit to be the eyes of your soul revealing the very things my fire must consume.

Day 29

Day 30

Separate
Matthew 13:24-30

Pay attention to what I am doing in this season. The time has come to separate the wheat from the tares. For a time, you have been allowed to grow together but now I must manifest my true Glory. Although you may look alike, there will be no mistaking the wheat that belongs to me. There will no longer be room for wolves to hide in the pasture. Your true nature will be revealed. You shall receive the inheritance that awaits your fruit. The influence of the tares is diminishing. My children shall bring light that illuminates all the subtleties of your ways. Awaken, oh son, for you have been asleep for so long. You are waiting on me to arise with power in my wings. The time is now, so stand with me as we declare my Glory.

Day 30

Day 31

I Have Called You Righteous
2 Corinthians 5:21

By Christ's blood you were ushered into right standing with me. I have called you unto myself, covering and sealing you with my grace, love, and peace. Shake off your old familiar nature because it has lost the power to rule you. It is powerless to bring about any more bondage in your life. You now bear my name, we are one, you in me and I in you. Now you must have the courage and boldness to stand in the place I have called you to. All I see when I look upon you is a vessel adorned with my beauty and light, fit to be in a place of royalty. I see beauty that surpasses all understanding. Do you know the perfection you were washed in? This has caused you to stand before me without spot or blemish. I have called you righteous, and righteous shall be your name.

Day 31

Day 32

The Unlocking of My Sons

Oh, you ancient doors and hidden wells, release the waters that I have hidden inside of you. Oh, what secrets and mysteries you contain. Have you forgotten my true intent towards you? It is to establish the identity of who I have called you to be. Have you forgotten the power that you possess? Unlock, you ancient doors, so that the King of Glory may come in. Awaken, King, Priest, Son, for that is who I have called you to be. Do you not know who you are? Majesty awaits you. Open your eyes that you may see and unstop your ears that you may hear. Creation has need of what you bring. I created you to occupy, dwell, rule and reign upon the earth. Come stand on the mountain so we may commune face to face. King to king walking in unity. I will stir your waters until they overflow their banks to relieve the cry of the nations. Let me unlock you. You will bring forth new life.

Day 32

Volume 3

What Shall I Manifest

Romans 8:22 says that the whole earth and creation has been moaning and groaning as they wait on the manifestation of the sons of God. I often would quote this verse as if I were waiting for some missing piece within me for the Lord to fulfill, not really understanding that in order for me to be a manifested son, God has given me everything that I need. For the past two years I have been on a journey to really understand what it means to be a son of God. You see, I have allowed much fruit to grow in my life that produced a harvest that did not always edify me. I have been stuck in depression, guilt, shame, but all the while walking in ministry. I have been speaking and teaching about a God who heals and makes people whole, everyone but me. I had a need to have everything look like I was okay and walking the exemplary walk with no faults, stumbling, or short comings, or insecurities. I could never walk and let you see that part of me because I didn't think that you would understand. I had to have it all together to fit with my position as a minister of the gospel.

Through this volume of the devotional, God is giving you a choice. You will identify places where you may have manifested some fruit that is not pleasing, but he wants us to get it right. Through grace and mercy, we have an opportunity to continue being transformed into that son. The truth is, as I said earlier, we are not waiting on God to do anything. Instead, he is waiting on us to wake up and realize we have all that we need on the inside of us to manifest his kingdom right where we are. At the end of each entry, I pose this question: What shall you manifest? As you receive what God is saying to you personally each day, journal the answers and strategy you come up with. Write the vision and make a plan. God is waiting on us to realize who we are and to understand our true identify and what we have on the inside of us. You are his solution; you are the answer the world is looking for. What shall you manifest?

Day 33

It is Time to be Revealed
1 Peter 1:5-8

I see you, my child, I see and know what you are going through. It amazes me when you can go through suffering with joy and peace and how you have courage and faith even when you cannot see or feel me nearby. You must remember you are forever surrounded by my light. You have my Glory. Even though you cannot see or touch me, you believe, and that is faith. Continue your song of praise and keep rejoicing. It is here where my Glory shall be revealed through you. What shall you manifest? Will you stand in power and authority? Greater works you have been called to fulfill. Open your mouth and establish my Kingdom.

Day 33

Day 34

Where Shall I Lay My Head?
Luke 9:58

I am looking for a resting place, for somewhere to lay my head. I am looking for a vessel that can activate my government on its shoulders, implementing rule and reign in the natural earth. Where shall I rest my head? Is it in you? Who shall manifest the atmosphere of heaven where they stand? The kingdom is looking for sons who will let me rest my government on their shoulders. I will teach you how to rule and legislate from this place. What shall you manifest?

Day 34

Day 35

You Are Light

I am inviting you into a mystery, the mystery of the Kingdom. Let me unlock it. Inside of you, you possess a light. If you allow me, I will reveal and illuminate it for all to see through you. Within this light all will find what they are searching for. It is here in this state of illumination you become the answer and can be all things to all men. Come close and commune with me and I will unlock each realm of my glory in you. What shall you manifest?

Day 35

Day 36

Be Sober
1 Peter 5:8

Keep watch as you build a house with me. The materials that you will use are praise and prayer. With these you will surely build a firm foundation, a dwelling place that no enemy will be able to penetrate even though your adversary is circling, looking for the smallest crack in your foundation to enter. Be sober in your thinking, speech, and motives. Walk soberly in love and allow all your flesh to be submitted to me. I will be your dwelling place, making you the beauty of all nations. What shall we manifest together?

Day 36

Day 37

Shift

The time has come for you to completely step into your destiny, holding nothing back. Now is the time the latter rain must meet the former rain. Supernatural children are what I desire in this hour. Shift now from your old way of thinking for I have created you as a living spirit housed in flesh. However, you are not flesh, you are supernatural. You have an ability within you that transcends time and space, or anything that has ever been done in the flesh. These are the gifts that I left for you to win the world. No longer focus on your trials or shortcomings. I, Jehovah Jireh, am your provider for everything you need. You lack nothing. Simply speak in faith and it will be established for you. Shift your mind, heart, and soul into my kingdom. Live in the Spirit and you will access more, for abundant life awaits. There is still yet a work that must be done through your hands. I can only do it if you seek me as your source. Just as I commanded the ravens to feed Elijah so have I made provision for you. It is your nature to doubt because the world says you get nothing for free, but freely I give to you all that I have. Can I be your everything, and share the mysteries of my kingdom with you? Shift into my spiritual life of abundance and favor that is chasing after you. Expect to see and experience the continuance of my presence as you ascend to where I am. Shift now, take me out of the box that you have housed me in so that I may break forth. What shall you manifest?

Day 37

Day 38

Sons Wanted
Matthew 20:26

I have chosen you and qualified you to lead. I have exalted you and given you my qualification of righteousness. Do not allow yourself to be put into a box but become a vessel that the master can use. Do not get caught up in titles or comparison for it will only lead you to destruction. You are what the earth has been groaning for as it longs for my voice to awaken. Now is the time you must activate your voice. I have chosen you to establish my kingdom. Walk in love and unity for those are the only keys that work. Only this will create a culture that cannot be stopped. What shall you manifest?

Day 38

Day 39

Come to Thy Father's House
Luke 15:11-22

I am patiently waiting for the Sons of God to arise. Stand in your rightful place. For I have given you an inheritance but many have misused it and allowed it to be wasted. Nevertheless, I am calling to you once again. Come into your
Father's house; my arms are open wide, ready to receive you once again. For I have covered your nakedness with my righteousness, establishing you and seating you in heavenly places. Come, my love, no condemnation awaits you but only my perfected love. Come into thy Father's house.
What shall you manifest?

Day 39

Day 40

Th Spirit of Cain
1 John 3:12

I must warn you of what I see in my bride. She cares more about how man sees her than me. She competes with her own family to receive all the glory. Be careful, my love, for there is a power influencing you that wishes to devour you. Its mission is to choke my light out, only leaving darkness. Remember you are all one; there is no one greater than the other. In unity we stand. Choose to eat of the food and drink I offer, rejecting any other delicacy. I honor those who honor me. I chase after those who earnestly seek me. You are enough, you are what I want now and forever. I will not always tolerate your ignorance. The time has come when your childish thoughts must be put away. Insecurities must be dealt with in the light of truth. Reject jealousy and pride. What shall you manifest?

Day 40

Day 41

Command the Sun to Stand Still
Joshua 10:12-14

Do you know who you are? What authority is upon you? There is power and authority in your tongue to shut up or loose the heavens on earth. So why are you defeated? Why is midnight still here? Command the sun, my child, to stand still, and forbid night to come until you have reached victory. Take courage that I am for you and your battle has already been won. No longer will you retreat; pursue your enemy until you have utterly destroyed his kingdom. Open your mouth and speak to your battle and declare victory. I have put fire in your mouth that will devour so submit to my will and I will give you the strategy to destroy your enemy. What shall you manifest?

Day 41

Day 42

Obligation
Matthew 15:8-9

I could care less about your traditions and religion simply because I can see your heart is far from me. You say you serve me, but what you really feel is obligation to the things you have built up in your life that represent me. It is your love that I am after. Where is your heart in the religious acts you do in my name? Where is your heart, my son? Works are never the way. Come away with me and learn who I AM. I AM is putting a demand on the things that have laid dormant and been wasted on the inside of you. I have called in to the depths of you to hear my call. No longer do you have to live without everything you need. I have made a way. Learn of me today, give me your heart and not just your service.

What shall you manifest?

Day 42

Day 43

Put on the New
Ephesians 4:22-32

Come commune with me, my child. I have something new for you. I want you to leave all the former things you have known. Join me here, now, and forever more. I will show you how to ascend to the place to which I have called you. A place that was created just for you. Step into the new, for here I have fashioned a new garment for you to wear. This garment will illuminate your true light. In this place everything that was made was made for you. It all belongs to you and if you speak it shall respond to your voice. There is no lack in this place; abundance rules the atmosphere. Will you come? Will you ascend? It is the only way to meet me face to face.

What shall you manifest?

Day 43

Day 44

Light up the World
Luke 8:16

I have ignited you; I choose you. Will you shine for me? Allow me to exalt you so that your light may be seen. I want to place you where your light will dispel all darkness. You will boldly shine for me. My purpose for you is to light up the world. What shall you manifest?

Day 44

Day 45

Passion
Zechariah 8:2

Where is your passion? My passion burns for you; it cannot be contained. My passion created Jesus as a sacrificial lamb for you and brought you back into right standing with me. What is it you are chasing? My Kingdom, my Glory? Or your own lust and ambitions? You shall receive your fruit. Let me ignite a fire that burns deep within you, that will cause you to follow hard after me. I will give you passion that you will not be able to contain. Turn toward me for it will cause you to pursue me in a new place. Extravagantly, enthusiastically, with full desire. I will become the object of your affection. Come run hard after me. What shall you manifest?

Day 45

Day 46

He Cannot Stop You
Acts 4:29-30

I have released favor for you to go and proclaim the year of the sovereign Lord. There is no force that can stop you or hold you back. All of heaven is available to you; go forth in boldness and proclaim the good news. Reconcile my children back to their Father in love. Every enemy in your path must bow because of what you carry inside. I have overcome it all. Every door and gate are open for you to go and fulfill what the scriptures have foretold. Greater works shall your hands produce. Now is the time when the latter rain will meet the former rain and produce a harvest that will surpass anything you have ever seen. You shall reign together. What shall you manifest?

Day 46

Day 47

I Will Visit
Numbers 14:18

Do you not know you have a new identity? The moment you stepped into my kingdom your bloodline changed. Guilt, shame, sin and iniquity no longer have any power over you. You have been adopted into my lineage of priest and kings. I need you to shut the door to some things that are trying to linger. For I have given you the keys to freedom and you are no longer bound by how you think you don't measure up. Everything within you has been made new and reset to my original design and blueprint. Rise king, rise priest, take your place, legislate in your sphere. No longer must you cower in the corner affected by the trauma of your past. I have made all things new. Every generational thing has been broken. You have a new name and are free from your past. Renew your mind and heart daily to declutter everything that will spoil your fruit. Seek me I will show you how to shut the door forever and walk in your new identity. What shall you manifest?

Day 47

Day 48

Pull Them Out
Jude 1:23

I have called you for this very hour. I have placed a breaker anointing on the inside of you, giving you access to dimensions and regions in prayer. You have become the gate and the door for those you stand in the gap for. Pull them into the place where I am. Stand as an oak to cover them and hide them from the rain. Intercede for my light to be revealed in them, casting out all darkness around them. I have truly called you to set those who are captive free. I will hear your prayer so align your heart with mine. Just as my son came for the sick and broken so shall you bring them to me. What shall you manifest?

Day 48

Day 49

I Will Take Egypt Out of You

You have already made your exodus, yet there is still something within you which hinders how I move through you. It is a mindset you have yet to cast down. Unless I reveal it, you cannot even detect it is there. Yes, I have called you out of Egypt. Now the chore is to get Egypt out of you. How is it that Egypt is in you, you say? In the way you talk, think, live, hear and see. You allow yourself to be enslaved to a system whose debt you cannot pay. You limit yourself by allowing Egypt to become master over your life. Listen to the Spirit of the Lord: "Your debt has been paid in full." Allow me to sever the roots of what Egypt planted in you. Take comfort in your wilderness for this is the ground where we establish working together in unity. Here is where the refiner's fire purifies all impurities. I am always willing to uphold my word. All you need to do is surrender and I will bring you to the crème de le crème. What shall you manifest?

Day 49

Day 50

I Allowed It
Isaiah 55:8

Am I a cruel God? There are some things you must walk through in order to reach purpose and destiny. Like any parent I want only the best for you. How can you learn without trial and error? Every trial and shortcoming can be used to build your trust in me. Sometimes I see where you are headed, and I allow it because experience becomes your best teacher. I have also equipped you with wisdom and everything you need. It is up to you to use it. Trust me, I am not surprised about anything in your life. Take heart in knowing the enemy can only go as far as I allow him to go. You are surrounded by my mighty right hand. It is in the struggle where you will learn how to trust me. What shall you manifest?

Day 50

Day 51

The Whole Earth
Isaiah 6:3

Slow down, sit back, take it all in. What do you see? The birds are singing their song, insects are buzzing all around. The sun sets high in the sky. The trees bow and wave at the wind. Do you see it? The beauty, the splendor of all that was made. By my hands this whole earth, yes, this whole earth was made. The whole earth is filled with my glory. Consider how I slung the stars in the sky, accenting the darkness with the moon. Beauty, splendor, and majesty you encounter every day. Why? Because the whole earth is filled with my glory. Take your time to see what I have made. See what my hands have created, for it is good. Now then, what shall you manifest?

Day 51

Day 52

Going To and Fro
2 Chronicles 16:9

I am searching, looking to see anything that looks like me in the realm of the earth. I am looking for those who carry the torch of the Lord and wield my sword. I am looking for a people who radiate with light and glory. Who will stand for me? Who will embody my likeness? I want to manifest fully through these willing vessels. You are my end time remnant who carries the latter rain. You will stand in my glory and power. We shall destroy the camp of the enemy. This house that I have built shall stand forever. What shall you manifest?

Day 52

Day 53

Judah
Ephesians 1:11-12

Even though you wear your armor you are still exposed. You do all the right things yet still you are defeated. Listen, I hear the sound of the enemy in your camp, and you are not prepared. You have the knowledge of your weapons but lack skill in using them. Judah, where is you praise? Use it to draw me near. When you open your mouth the sound echoes through heaven producing what you need. I, with the host of heaven, will draw near. War with your praise and the enemy will flee. Shift the very atmosphere of war. Stay out of the valley of murmuring and complaint and use a sound mind to manifest exactly what you need. Everything you need is in you. What shall you manifest?

Day 53

Day 54

Seasons

I am now thrusting you into a new season with a deeper dimension of my love. Come walk with me from glory to glory. I know you thought I have been absent; maybe you even thought I had forgotten about you. The truth is I have never left your side. You must press past what you see to find me. This season shall be greater than the last. You shall receive a great harvest if you do not faint. Take courage, I have given you every tool you need. Seek me and you shall see victory. My kingdom has been placed on the inside of you. People are looking to you to show them a better way. Point them back to me. I will speak through you boldly if you lend yourself to my will. What shall you manifest?

Day 54

Day 55

More Than
Romans 8:37

You are not just a conqueror; you are more than that. The victory always belongs to you; your name is victory. You are more than an overcomer, and you stood when you wanted to give up. You have overcome it all with the blood of the Lamb and the word of your testimony. You have been tried and proven through faith; you now possess the keys to my kingdom. Step into the wealthy place and reign with me. You are more than a conqueror. What shall you manifest?

Day 55

Day 56

Who Can Separate?
Romans 8:38-39

I love you, but I have this against you. Why have you forgotten to seek me with your whole heart? You are no longer a sinner; I have changed your name to son. Do not be fooled but stay vigilant and keep watch because sin is always lurking at the door. Death only has the power you allow it to have in your life. The fact of the matter is the only way you can be separated from me is by your own will. Not by the enemy but rather, it is the choices you make. Sit at my table and eat for I will fill you with all that you need. What shall you manifest?

Day 56

Day 57

I Did It for You

Have you ever loved someone so much that you would give up anything for them? Sacrifice yourself just to save them? This is how my passion burns toward you. I gave of myself that you may be saved, I paid the ultimate sacrifice for you to be free. I encourage you today to cherish the intimacy we share and closeness you feel with me nearby. You have been given back what Adam lost in the garden; you now lack no good thing. I am pleading with you today: do not take this life for granted. The price I paid was high, but worth everything to see you restored and reconciled to me. All things are new, nothing remains from your adamic nature. Step into the place of a son. What shall you manifest?

Day 57

Day 58

Who Can Stand?
Romans 9:31

I, Jehovah, am for you; I prosper you to walk in dominion and favor over this earth. I stand in the gap to encourage and strengthen you. So, take joy in me today, for truly the joy of the Lord is in you. Commit yourself to learn of me in a new way. I will show you treasures and mysteries. You have entered a place of brokenness but now I, Jehovah, shall mold all the broken pieces together. The enemy thought he destroyed what I made, but I have sustained all of you. I can work my will through you and my fire will consume all that remains until you come forth as pure gold. I will show you who I am. You will stand assured that I am on your side and that no power above or beneath will be able to stand against you. What shall you manifest?

Day 58

Day 60

Subdue and Take the Land
Genesis 1:28

The blessing and order, which was given in the garden, have been restored. Take courage; subdue and take the land. You must take authority over all the high places, principalities, air waves, and the earth. For my kingdom is here. Now is the time to reign in authority and justice. For the earth has need of you. I am calling my warriors to march and reclaim areas that have been lost and lay desolate. I have silenced your enemy so watch him flee. My kingdom has come, so watch as I change the hearts of man. I have exalted you to reign with me. Come stand in your rightful place as I bring deliverance in my wings. Now the work of the kingdom shall be complete. Through your hands all glory and majesty will work to restore all who are broken, and they will return to me.

What shall you manifest?

Day 60

Day 61

Walk Into
Deuteronomy 8:1-10

The time has come for promotion. I have tried you through the fire, and yet you still stand. You have kept the faith in the wilderness. You have sown greatly yet reaped a small harvest. Now I open the windows of heaven and pour out a blessing too large to receive it all. I am planting in a new land with fertile soil and it shall yield a hundred-fold. A land flowing with abundance; never again shall you see lack. Keep me first for this land has all the resources you need. Walk into this land. What shall I manifest?

Day 61

Day 62

Without a Vision
Proverbs 29:19

Do you not remember that through the voice of my prophet, I told you to write the vision? You wonder why you are not prospering, when as my child, prosperity is in you. I have given you visions and dreams, yet you have not accepted any of them. Why are you waiting on me when I have already given them to you? What do you have in your hand? Stop waiting on my hand to do what has already been done. Get before me with pen and paper and I will bring strategy to unlock what is on the inside of you. What shall you manifest?

Day 62

Day 63

New Wine
Luke 5:35-39

I desire to give you new wine. This wine has been withheld for the latter rain. With this new wine you will be able to endure what is coming. You can stand sure-footed as a warrior in my army. What you must do now is put that old man to death. Renew your mind often to avoid traps and pitfalls along the way. Step into the new creation; I will fill you with new wine. What shall you manifest?

Day 63

Day 64

Authority
Romans 13:1-3

I exalt those whom I want. Authority comes from me; all things happen to accomplish my will. Nothing that happens comes as a surprise to me. I rain on the just and unjust. I exalt kings and leadership comes from me. Never question but pray for those in leadership over you. Stop judging and destroying them with your tongue. Not all your leaders have my heart, yet there is still purpose in that. Trust that I am God, I know what I am doing. In due time all will be revealed. What shall you manifest?

Day 64

Day 65

Idle Words
Matthew 12:36

Put a guard over your mouth. I am keeping watch over what words your tongue brings to life. Did you not know that the power of life and death lies in your tongue? With this member you can set your whole world ablaze. How long shall I consider your foolishness? You know what is good and right. You murder your brother with your tongue. You speak death instead of life. Submit your tongue to me; ask me to keep watch for you. I shall show you a more excellent way. What shall I manifest?

Day 65

Day 66

Followers Wanted
Matthew 7:23

There are some who say they belong to me and follow me. However, to me they are just fans. What is the difference between a fan and follower? A fan will cheer you on and even be in your corner; they even have a bit of loyalty to you. But a follower is the one whom I seek. A follower goes beyond a fan and learns the art of serving. They understand it is not enough just to be on the team. Sometimes sacrifices must be made and following won't always be comfortable. They do not have pride, but wear humility as a garment. These are the ones I seek, who will follow me no matter the cost. What shall I manifest?

Day 66

Day 67

Choose Life
Dueteronomy 30:11-20

Why do you question my love for you?
Why is every trial you go through my fault?
The answer is you do not really know me. Have I not told you I cause everything to work out for your good?
You focus on the problem and sink deeper and deeper into despair. Have you forgotten I gave you authority to control and rule? Are you living by my sovereign will for your life? If so hold on because I am with you and will never leave. You can endure so seek my face and you will find strength to stand. Choose life. It is so simple, my child. Follow me and reap an abundant harvest and receive your inheritance. What shall you manifest?

Day 67

Day 68

Spirit and Truth
John 24:4

It is time for you to walk in who you really are. I am revealing your true image to you if you will allow. You are so much more than what your natural eye can see. Spirit, soul, and body. A triune being magnificently divine in nature. You understand how to walk and be led of your flesh. However, submit to the spirit man who lives on the inside of you. Strengthen him and allow him to lead the way. He understands and hears my voice. He will lead you to truth. Stay connected to me as I transform you from glory to glory, changing the very reflection you see. The flesh tells of your shortcomings and what you can never be. The Spirit shows you the truth of who and what I have called you. Who shall you empower? Who shall you believe? What then shall you manifest?

Day 68

Day 69

Open Heavens

Hello, my child, what is it that you have need of? There is nothing that I will withhold from you. Simply speak and receive because you live under an open heaven. You are an heir to my throne and favor chases after you. Understand this: I have given you everything you need for you to complete your destiny. Jehovah Jireh has provided everything. Walk the rest of your journey under this open heaven. Speak my truth, teach my righteousness. What shall you manifest?

Day 69

Day 70

He is Here
Psalm 22:3

When you create an atmosphere of praise, it draws me near to you. When I hear the sound of Judah, you have my full attention. I love to inhabit my people as they usher in my Shekinah Glory to rest. Just my presence alone makes everything right. Let us become intimate so that I can show you what love is all about. Allow me to be the lover of your soul. Let us grow together for you will never be alone. I am here, always and forever. Never worry for I will never reject you; my love validates you. What shall you manifest?

Day 70

Day 71

"Issachar", Where are You?

I have placed an ability in you to testify of my dispensation of time. You know the next move of God. I have exalted you to sound the alarm. My kingdom has come to this earth to mirror heaven. Now is the time that I must separate the wheat and the tare. No longer will you be allowed to grow together. Which side shall you choose? Awaken to the mysteries that have been placed on the inside of you. I am speaking and revealing the days to come. You will know exactly what is on the horizon. Look within and find the answers you need. What shall you manifest?

Day 71

Day 72

To the Unknown God
Acts 17:23-31

Why am I still a stranger to you? What is it about me and my kingdom you do not believe? I am constantly drawing you, but you do not respond to me. You are constantly bogged down by the weight of your circumstances. What is this distance between you and me? I am alive, I am not some voiceless idol like other things in your life. I want to declare my name to you, “I AM”. I AM, because I am able to do all things. I am before all things and have made all things. Step into the realm of my presence and never thirst again. What shall you manifest?

Day 72

Day 73

My God Shall Supply
Philippians 4:19

I see how you sow and sacrifice so that my kingdom might prosper. You have sown in love, encouragement, words of wisdom, time, and money to those who are broken and hurting. You have given of yourself even when you had nothing to give. I will honor you for putting my kingdom first. I will open this window of heaven and pour out a blessing over you. I will entrust you with the treasures of heaven. Every need you have shall be supplied according to my riches.

Day 73

Day 74

Snake Bites
Galatians 5:15

You have ingested his venom and now it is killing you slowly. Bitterness, pride, and hatred are the fruit. You never address or deal with the venom, therefore, the issue becomes bigger than it really is. It travels through your being and affects every area it touches, leaving its destruction behind. It becomes unforgiveness. What do you do now? Where do you turn? Choose me, my child, for you were never meant to carry a burden like this. Choose love, and it will remove every roadblock obscuring your heart. Choose to forgive and the pain will go away. Give it to me for I know how much snake bites hurt, and I am the ultimate healer of all things. I can and will heal you if you ask. What shall you manifest?

Day 74

Day 75

Manifesting

You say you love me, but where do I fit into your life? You come for power and deliverance only to walk away in more bondage. I am being placed on the back burner and our work together is no longer important. You are not interested in me, but only what my hand can provide. Your heart is slowly fading away. It is being lulled to sleep by things that I created that you have allowed to become a distraction. You miss the clarity of my voice calling out to you. Consider who I have created you to be. You have the glory of I AM living on the inside of you. You are waiting for what I have already done; you are lost in the middle of nowhere moving fast. Slow down, come back, join my table. Let me change what you crave. Seek my Son so you can manifest your full authority as king and priest. What I say shall stand. What shall we manifest?

Day 75

Day 76

Just Jump In

Open your mind. How is it ruling you? Within you, you can find the solution to anything. It is not my fault you choose to live this way. I have given you access. Listen, you have failed to seek my council. You seek those who only see part of the picture and not the whole canvas. If you could truly see, you would know that all things are bowing at your feet and waiting on you to tell them what they should be. Get off the riverbank where it is safe and comfortable. Just jump in--what are you waiting for? Live in the present for this is your time. Jump off the cliff and soar, ascending to new heights in me. I have much I long to show you. Live with abandon and trust fully in my ability to sustain you. It does not have to make sense. You are not waiting on my time to move. I am waiting on you to realize the time is now. What shall you manifest?

Day 76

Day 77

Like a Flood
Psalm 24:7-10

I am coming, flowing like a mighty river. You have asked me to come. I will destroy the walls that separate me from you. I am riding on the wings of grace, mercy, splendor and might. I have utterly destroyed the works of the enemy. Now I will drown out his lies and open your eyes to the light of truth. I will submerge you in my river until you are overtaken. Stand and see the salvation of the Lord. What shall you manifest?

Day 77

Day 78

I Will Give You Rest
Matthew 11:28-30

Come in, all who are weary, for I will give you rest. Cast your burdens at my feet and I will carry them now. I have given you an invitation to my kingdom, so enter in and you shall find rest. Come, let me take all that has made you heavy. I can handle it. In turn I will give you rest. What shall you manifest?

Day 78

Day 79

Be Patient
2 Timothy 2:24-26

You be the bearer of truth so that you can instruct and direct your brother into all truth. Love and honor him to the point where I may be revealed to him. Have you forgotten where I brought you from? Stand firm in my love; do not waver. Do not judge or backbite. Put a watch over your mouth and stop murdering your brother by the words that you speak. How can I bless what you curse? See through the lens of my sight. You are all a part of a beautiful woven tapestry still under construction. Be patient in what you cannot see yet in others for I am working on the root. It is yet to be revealed what they shall be. What shall you manifest?

Day 79

Day 80

Kingship
Revelation 1:5-6

Do you really know who I have called you to be? You are king and priest. Not the president, CEO, manager, mother, father, son, or daughter. A nation of kings and priests. You must learn your identity and leave behind who you thought you were. Step into your kingship and allow the Holy Spirit to teach you how to reign and serve in my kingdom. Position yourself between me and humanity so you can become all things to all men. Grow up into this mighty call, so that you may rule and reign forever. What shall you manifest?

Day 80

Day 81

Intrepid Warrior

I am in search of a warrior; here are the qualifications: You must be fearless and dauntless. You cannot have a double mind. I need a warrior who believes that in every battle he is victorious. A warrior who is not afraid to enter the hidden and dark places and bring the light. One who is not swayed by what he sees but stands on what he knows. Is this you? Are you the one? My eyes are scouring this earth for someone. Come to me make and yourself known, for there is much to teach you. I will train and equip you to stand. I have sounded the alarm; will you answer the call? What shall you manifest?

Day 81

Day 82

I Will Blow on It
Ephesians 3:20

What are your dreams? What are your plans? Everything you have tried in one way or another has ended in ruins. How can you manifest what you have no vision to see? Use your imagination, can you see it? Now speak what you see, call it into time and space to rest in this dimension. You were built to live a life of abundance for my seed never begs for bread. Whatever you are establishing I will blow my breath upon. Watch it multiply, watch it flourish and become the thing you intend it to be. Exceedingly abundantly above all you can ask or think. What shall you manifest?

Day 82

Day 83

Shipwrecked
1 Timothy 1:18-20

What has my Spirit prophesied? Has it manifested? Are you walking in it? For prophecy to work you have a major part to play. You are not waiting on me to fulfill it for that was done when Jesus died on the cross. Seek me for the strategy, ask me for the vision if you have none. I will give it to you in abundance. You first must see it. The grave is full of those who never fulfilled their destinies or my purpose for their life. I want to manifest everything that has been foretold about you. Help further my kingdom. I have placed ideas and callings inside of you that must be birthed. I have held up my end of the deal. Now it is up to you to seek and submit to my will. Every door will be open to you, so if you have found yourself shipwrecked, come back to me and I will re-ignite your flame. I will set you on fire once again to burn for me. What shall you manifest?

Day 83

Day 84

The High Place

Come up higher to another dimension. Experience a place in me you have never been. You will never know my vastness completely. Once you think you have come to the end of me, I will open another realm of glory. Come travel with me and move from glory to glory. There is depth that you have not even began to step into. Only if you allow me will I overtake you. Come to the high place with me because there is so much I want to show you. There is no room for struggle in this place, for here you see as I see. Nothing is hidden from you here; come go with me. What shall you manifest?

Day 84

Day 85

Are You Willing?

Open your heart, my child. You have asked me to come and protect you, but I have found walls that surround you. Unless you allow me to break through, I can't come. I want to fill you, but how can I fill something that is already full? Empty yourself of all worry, stress, and fear. I will fill you with an everlasting love. You have asked me to sit on the throne of your heart, but how can I if that seat is filled with you? Step down and let me reign there forever. You are controlled by your own lust; surrender now and I will come in like a mighty rushing wind. What shall you manifest?

Day 85

Day 86

Live
Romans 8:1-17

I have given you the key, now possess it and live. If you continue after the law surely you will die. Press, my child, allow my spirit to live in you. Therefore, continue with righteousness and abounding love. Come live with me, come reign with me. Come out of slavery, step into the light of freedom. What shall you manifest?

Day 86

Day 87

Slay Goliath

I am seeking a warrior who hates what I hate and loves what I love. Someone like David who will take a stand and slay Goliath. You have giants in the field. I need you to realize that with my love, power, and authority you can overcome anything. Are you a world changer? One who will fearlessly stand in the face of the giant and not be moved? What shall you manifest?

Day 87

Day 88

I Will Show You the Way Out

I do not want you to fail, and I have given you every chance to find me. I take no pleasure in your pain. Every time you hurt, I hurt. I created you to be more than a conqueror. You are worth more than you think you are. I created you in three parts. Spirit, soul, and body, now ruled from the inside. I have shown you the way out; come through the blood. Accept my invitation. What shall you manifest?

Day 88

Day 89

What Is Your Confession?

Do you not realize you're standing in the fruit of what your words and thoughts have framed? What is swirling around you? Your atmosphere was created by you. What do you confess? What comes out of your mouth? Let me tell you a secret you are whilst we speak. Whether it be good or bad, your tongue activates your thoughts. So, I ask you once again, what is your confession? What shall you manifest?

Day 89

Day 90

Time Is Almost Out

In a moment, in a twinkling of an eye, I am come with my reward. How shall I find you? Have you prepared for your groom? Do you eagerly await my arrival? Will I find you radiating with my glory? Or will you be in darkness with your light snuffed out? For night is coming and no man will be able to work. What condition will your heart be in? Full of peace and love or every detestable thing? I am coming for my bride. What reward shall you receive? How will I find you when I come? What shall you manifest?

Day 90

Day 91

Sound the Alarm
Joel 2

Sound the alarm. I am calling you, awakening you to come to me. Can you feel me drawing you? This path is full of my favor. I need you here in rank and file and order for I have need of you. Stay connected with my legion remnant in this hour because they surely know the way. How do you find them? Stand still and listen for they are releasing a sound that will quicken every part of you. The time is near get into your position and wait for my command. What shall you manifest?

Day 91

Day 92

Relentless
1 Kings 18:24

I am looking for my relentless sons who will never give up on me. Those who will follow me anywhere no matter what the test. Is that you? In order to make it in this last hour you must have a tenacity that never gives up. I shall not fail you; the time has passed for the reign of the double minded man. Life has profited him nothing. Choose today who you will be. What shall you manifest?

Day 92

Day 93

Laodicea
Rev. 3:14-22

Look at all you have gained and made for yourself. So successful, the envy of all. You think you have arrived, but you do not know how truly pitiful you are. All you have gained has cost you a heavy penalty. The more you get the less that hunger on the inside is satisfied. You may fool your brother, but I, your God, know your true nature. Place yourself back on the altar and become my servant because I long to say "Well done, good and faithful servant." My fire will consume and devour your flesh. I will change your garment into humility. What shall you manifest?

Day 93

Day 94

The Path
Matt. 7: 13-14

You say you want to stay in my Presence, but there is only one way you can. You must stay on the narrow path. It is not easy or comfortable and you may endure suffering. Trust and believe in me because there is nothing impossible with me. This path leads you to death, because first you must die in order to live in me. What shall you manifest?

Day 94

Day 95

What Is Love?
Isaiah 53:3-12

What is love? It is not boastful nor selfish. It is not proud but humble and meek and it never ends. It is full of passion and sacrifice. It has the power to save, deliver, and heal. Many claim to have it but are fooled by the counterfeit. As freely as you give you shall receive. Love considers not its own and gives all it has without limitation. Over and over, it renews itself, generating more energy and power to sustain. Choose to be intentional. Choose to love unconditionally. What shall you manifest?

Day 95

Day 96

Are You Emotional or Passionate?

I see that you are moved by what you see. I see how my word touches and comforts you. Have you really caught the revelation of what I am saying? Press past your emotions and let me ignite passion in you. What you feel is always fleeting, however, what you know and believe frames your world. Have you found yourself in the same cycle over and over again? One day you are sure, the next all hope is lost. Take control and rule your emotions for you have dominion. I have never changed, I am always the same. You are safe with me. My right hand will never fail to hold you up. Redirect you gaze and you shall see all things for nothing is hidden from you. What shall you manifest?

Day 96

Day 97

Living in the New
Hebrews 5:12

Anticipation is building.
Everything is responding to the buzz of my kingdom come. You are stepping into a new era in time. A time that has been held back for this time and day. You are living in the era of the sons of God. Can you feel the energy surging through the air? Creation is responding to what you say. Fulfillments of all have been set in place. Righteous, you stand in authority. Rule, king, speak, priest, and manifest my glory, son. Continue to press and align with my will. In your hands I have given you the power of death and life. Build and establish whatever there is in your heart to do. What shall you manifest?

Day 97

Day 98

Throw the Covers Back

I see you even when you try to cover the acts of your hand. Throw the covers back, open your heart. Come wash in my blood and become white as snow. Let us bring everything to the light for it is here you get clarity. Nothing can hide when it is exposed to my light, the light which make all darkness flee. Wash in my blood. Look at you standing there looking brand new. Shame and guilt no longer have a place to land. Come closer, get intimate with me. What shall you manifest?

Day 98

Day 99

You Are Worth It

I have called you worthy and righteous in my sight. It was my good pleasure to redeem you and bring you back to me. You are swimming in a pool of false humility. Sin is no longer an issue for you can choose to engage or not. Your life is dependent on the fruit you produce. This invisible chain that holds you has no power over you. Step forward into my grace. Let me correct the lie you tell yourself, that you will never measure up. I choose you and will continue to choose you. Dare to believe what I say about you. What shall you manifest?

Day 99

Day 100

Dripping with Oil

There is a fountain that flows, a place where you can come. You will continually be in my presence and I have invited you to live here. Step into the flow; I have given you access to my oil. Here you will become all things to all men. They will seek you out for the oil that flows from you. Oil that will keep their lamps full as it lights their path. Are you ready? Can you feel the anticipation of my glory? I ask you, son, what shall you manifest?

Day 100

Day 101

New Wine

I am creating a new vessel of honor. It is without holes or cracks. No longer will what I put into you leak out. I will age it to maturity. Those who are thirsty will come and drink of this new wine. In order for you to possess its power do not give up in the time of crushing. A new day is dawning for the son is rising. What shall you manifest?

Day 101

Day 102

Already Loved

You are almost home so do not quit. Why are you standing at such a distance from me? I have loved you before you even knew what love was. I saw all of you and still choose the cross. Come out of hiding; you are safe here with me. Can you accept my love? Will you stay in my love? Will you allow my love to heal your wounds? There is no need to seek for what you already have. I have loved you since before you knew you were loved. So, what then shall you manifest?

Day 102